Gordon Streisand

111 Places
in Miami and the Keys
That You Must
Not Miss

emons:

© Emons Verlag GmbH
All rights reserved
Photographs © Gordon Streisand, except:
page 21, photo courtesy of Area 31;
page 75, photo courtesy of Rob O'Neal;
page 115, photo courtesy of Coral Reef Park Company
© Cover icon: iStockphoto.com/Jan-Otto
Design: Eva Kraskes, based on a design
by Lübbeke | Naumann | Thoben
Edited by Katrina Fried
Maps: altancicek.design, www.altancicek.de
Printing and binding: B.O.S.S Medien GmbH, Goch
Printed in Germany 2016
ISBN 978-3-95451-644-5
Revised second edition, April 2016

Did you enjoy it? Do you want more?
Join us in uncovering new places around the world on:
www.111places.com

Foreword

In a city where not many people have deep roots, I'm proud to say my family's called Miami home since 1950, when my great-grandfather moved his wife and kids from Pittsburgh to a sleepy beach town in South Florida that offered sun, fun, and beautiful scenery. Growing up less than an hour north of Miami, I made the city and its environs my stomping grounds from the moment I was old enough to stomp. My grandmother showed me the Venetian Pool, a frequent hangout when she was young, in Coral Gables. She told me about her parents' home in Lower Matecumbe, the popular weekend getaway where she and her family would buy stone crabs from their neighbor for a dollar a pound. My mother often took me to the Parrot Jungle, now known as Pinecrest Gardens, where she used to work and eventually got married, just minutes from her childhood home. My father introduced me to the splendor of Biscayne Bay on his old Hobie Cat, sometimes tipping the boat for a thrill. My friends and I still peruse records at Sweat before we head to a Marlins game, having a drink or three at their Clevelander before first pitch.

The journeys to Miami and the Keys were an adventure, a pilgrimage, and a homecoming, all wrapped up into one. From stumbling upon the technicolor interior of the Bacardi Building to having vivid flashbacks of frolicking on Crandon Park beach as a little kid, I was continuously reminded of how Miami has both stayed the same and transformed dramatically over the past few decades. Handfuls of skyscrapers appear to pop up weekly on the skyline. The Keys used to be a quirky cluster of islands predominantly inhabited by fishermen. Today, multimillion-dollar homes line the shores from Key Largo to Key West. Amid the old and new are an untold number of hidden treasures and pleasures – places and stories that reveal Miami's true character, spirit, and above all, moxie. I hope you'll enjoy visiting them as much I have enjoyed rediscovering them.

111 Places

1___ African Queen
Rickety cinema royalty | 10

2___ Alabama Jack's
Low key in the Keys | 12

3___ Amertec Building
Hialeah's abandoned alien | 14

4___ Ancient Spanish Monastery
Medieval Spain in Miami | 16

5___ Anne's Beach
Florida's best rest stop | 18

6___ Area 31
Happy hour with a view | 20

7___ Atlantis Condominiums
Miami Vice lives on | 22

8___ Bahia Honda
Sleep with the fishes | 24

9___ Bay of Pigs Museum
A tragedy remembered | 26

10___ Betsy the Giant Lobster
If only she was on the menu … | 28

11___ Big Cypress Gallery
Ansel Adams of the Everglades | 30

12___ Bill Baggs Cape Florida State Park
Solitude by the city | 32

13___ Black Point Marina
Sea cow sanctuary | 34

14___ Blue Hole
Freshwater oasis in a saltwater desert | 36

15___ Boca Chita Key
Paradise found | 38

16___ Brickell Soccer Rooftop
Fútbol in the financial district | 40

17___ The Calle Ocho Walk of Fame
Looking down at the stars | 42

18___ Cat Man
Not a dog-and-pony show | 44

19___ Cauley Square
All aboard the kitsch caboose | 46

20___ CIFO Tile Facade
Downtown's bamboo forest | 48

21___ City Hall
Seaplanes and city managers | 50

22___ Clevelander at Marlins Park
Poolside in left field | 52

23___ Club Nautico
See Miami in its element | 54

24___ Coconut Grove Playhouse
Part cinema, all history | 56

25___ Coppertone Girl
Moon over Miami | 58

26___ Coral Castle
A fortress built to mend a broken heart | 60

27___ Crandon Park Zoo
Free-range peacocks and iguanas | 62

28___ Cuba Tobacco Cigar Co.
Up in smoke on Calle Ocho | 64

29___ Deering Estate
Poor man's Vizcaya | 66

30___ Domino Park
Playing by the numbers | 68

31___ El-Carajo
Stop for the gas, stay for the food, take home the wine | 70

32___ El Palacio de los Jugos
Cold drink hot spot | 72

33___ Ernest Hemingway's Cats
For whom the cat meows | 74

34___ Española Way
Pedestrian paradise | 76

35___ Fireman Derek's Key Lime Pie
Set your taste buds ablaze | 78

36___ Florida Keys Brewing Company
Ice cold in Islamorada | 80

37___ Florida Keys Wild Bird Rehabilitation Center
Wings on the mend | 82

38___ Fruit & Spice Park
Fruit, spice, and everything nice | 84

39   Los Gallos of Calle Ocho
Cuban humility | 86

40   Green Turtle Inn
Sid and Roxie's Islamorada institution | 88

41   Greynolds Park
Miami's Mount Everest | 90

42   Hanging Gardens at Perez Art Museum
Babylon by the bay | 92

43   Haulover Cut
The gateway to Miami's watershed | 94

44   Hialeah Park
The sport of kings for those who aren't | 96

45   History of Diving Museum
20,000 leagues into the Keys | 98

46   HM69 Nike Missile Base
On the brink of world destruction | 100

47   Holocaust Memorial
Hand of God | 102

48   I-95 Express Lanes
You get what you pay for | 104

49   Ichimura Japanese Garden
Secret sanctuary on Watson Island | 106

50   InterContinental's Dancer
Hold me closer light-up dancer | 108

51   Jackie Gleason's Mausoleum
Ralph Kramden's last stop | 110

52   The Jewel Box
Elevator to heaven | 112

53   John Pennekamp Coral Reef State Park
Underwater playground | 114

54   Key West Cemetery
Laugh to death | 116

55   Knaus Berry Farm
All buns go to heaven | 118

56   Lincoln Road Garage
Miami's parking chateau | 120

57   Lock & Load
Say hello to my little friend | 122

58   Locust Projects
A young artist's nursery | 124

59   Lou La Vie
Cruise Miami like a celebrity | 126

60   Mack's Fish Camp
The last of the Gladesmen | 128

61   Mary's Coin Laundry
Wash, fold, drink, repeat | 130

62   Matheson Hammock
A beginner's beach | 132

63   McAlpin Hotel
Quintessential Art Deco | 134

64   Mel Fisher Maritime Museum
Today's the day | 136

65   Metromover
Miami's monorail | 138

66   Miami Auto Museum
The city's grandest carport | 140

67   Miami Catamarans
Sailing solace | 142

68   Miami Circle
Ancient ruins in a modern jungle | 144

69   Miami Club Rum
South Beach's sustenance | 146

70   Miami Jai-Alai
The "world's fastest game" | 148

71   Miami Marine Stadium
Beautiful urban blight | 150

72   Mitzi's Memorial
R.I.P. Flipper | 152

73   Monkey Jungle
Catching up with your ancestors | 154

74   National Key Deer Refuge
Bambi's baby brothers and sisters | 156

75   News Cafe
People-watching paradise | 158

76   O Cinema
Popcorn and circumstance | 160

77   Ochopee Post Office
Littlest house on the prairie | 162

78   Old Cutler Road
Banyan-covered bliss | 164

79 Old Planetarium
Retro planetary retrograde | 166

80 Oleta River State Park
Row into the city | 168

81 Orion Herbs
Miami's medicine man | 170

82 Panther Coffee
You're not in Starbucks anymore | 172

83 Perky's Bat Tower
Mosquito mishap | 174

84 Pinecrest Gardens
Bye bye birdies | 176

85 Rickenbacker Causeway
Feel the burn | 178

86 Robbie's
Fish feeding frenzy | 180

87 Robert is Here
The little farm stand that could | *182*

88 Robert the Doll
Before there was Chucky, there was Robert | 184

89 Schnebly Redland's Winery
No grapes necessary | 186

90 Shark Valley
Everglades from above | 188

91 Shell World
They sell seashells by the seashore | 190

92 Skunk Ape Research Headquarters
Return of the Yeti | 192

93 Skyline from Watson Island
A city on the rise | 194

94 Skyward Kites
Go fly a kite | 196

95 South Pointe Park
Sittin' on the dock of Biscayne Bay | 198

96 Southernmost Point
So they say … | 200

97 Staircase to Nowhere
The Fontainebleau's folly | 202

98 Stiltsville
Square feet or square fathoms? | 204

99   Stone Barge at Vizcaya
Party on a pirate ship | 206

100   Sunken Garden
Hidden beauty at Fairchild Tropical Gardens | 208

101   Sunrise at Crandon Park
Good morning, South Florida | 210

102   Sweat Records
Vinyl and vegan | 212

103   Theater of the Sea
Sea-life spectacle | 214

104   Venetian Pool
The emerald of Coral Gables | 216

105   Versailles
A tale of two restaurants | 218

106   Virginia Key Beach Park
The long arm of Jim Crow | 220

107   Wallcast
An orchestra for the everyman | 222

108   Wat Buddharangsi
Serenity now | 224

109   Wolfsonian
Mediterranean marshmallow | 226

110   Wood Tavern's Bathrooms
Art surrounds the throne | 228

111   World Erotic Art Museum
The Smithsonian of kink | 230

1 African Queen

Rickety cinema royalty

One of the most treasured pieces of American movie history sits docked in the canals of Key Largo. In the shadows of a Holiday Inn, a few steps below a gravel parking lot on the side of US 1, the small, rickety wooden *African Queen* – the same vessel that Humphrey Bogart and Katharine Hepburn navigated through the leech-infested waterways of German East Africa – sits idly tied to a couple of wood posts. Other than a small brown sign on the main road that points to its location and a friendly man at the dock who greets you, no fanfare surrounds the boat.

Unlike most movies of its time, *The African Queen* wasn't shot in front of a painted background in a Hollywood studio. Instead, it was filmed on location in the Belgian Congo, an extremely rare feat for 1951. The production was also one of the few instances revered film critic and author James Agee collaborated on a script, helping craft the perfect climax for *The African Queen* – for which Bogart won his only Academy Award, beating out Marlon Brando's iconic performance in *A Streetcar Named Desire*.

The boat itself was built in turn-of-the-century England for the East Africa British Railways company, crafted to shuttle cargo, missionaries, and hunting parties across the Victoria Nile and Lake Albert, around the border of Uganda and the Belgian Congo. After making her famous silver-screen debut in 1951, the boat remained in Africa until 1968, eventually making her way to the States to work for charter operations on the West Coast and in Florida. In 1982, attorney and film buff Jim Hendricks found the *African Queen* decaying in a cow pasture near Gainesville, bought it for $65,000, and made it seaworthy. Today, the storied boat takes people from the heart of Key Largo out to the Atlantic Ocean and back every two hours, from ten in the morning until six at night, allowing fans to live out their fantasies of Hollywood's Golden Age.

Address 99701 Overseas Highway, Key Largo, 33037 FL, +1 305.451.8080, www.africanqueenflkeys.com | Hours Daily 10am–6pm | Tip Visit the Caribbean Club (104080 Overseas Hwy), the inspiration for another famous cinema classic, *Key Largo*. Its exterior was featured in the film, which starred Humphrey Bogart and Lauren Bacall.

2 Alabama Jack's

Low key in the Keys

In the middle of brackish wetlands, where the Everglades gets its pinch of salt, lies Card Sound Road, a small two-lane thoroughfare that runs from Florida City to the northern end of Key Largo. Only an experienced traveler or someone very skilled with Google Maps would opt to take this narrow, scenic route, off the beaten path of US 1. The surroundings alone make it the worth the drive, but another reward awaits. Halfway between the mainland and Key Largo, floating among the mangrove-covered islands, is Alabama Jack's, serving "Downtown Card Sound's" most delicious morsels since the early 1950s.

Just before arriving at the bridge to North Key Largo, a roadside bar with a row of parked Harleys out front welcomes one and all. A mix of bikers, locals, families, and adventurous visitors flocks to this open-air outpost complete with wooden floors, metal tables, and plastic cutlery. The sun bounces off the murky waters on the south side of Alabama Jack's as small fishing boats pass by throughout the day. Keep your eyes peeled for a glimpse of an alligator or crocodile in the water, as the bar is in the middle of their breeding grounds.

Old, battered license plates adorn the beams that run across the ceiling, over the bar serving up old-fashioneds, and into the kitchen, where the best conch fritters in the state are deep-fried and plated. Settle in at a table while the Jimmy Buffett cover band rocks out a rendition of "Margaritaville," and enjoy a heaping golden-brown basket of conch. Tartar and cocktail sauces accompany the crispy and fluffy fritters, topped with a fresh slice of Florida lime. Bell peppers, sweet onions, and Old Bay seasoning bring the batter and conch to life, rather than overwhelm the flavor as many fish shacks tend to do. Wash it down with a frosty mug of domestic beer and watch the sun set into the thickets from the county line.

Address 58000 Card Sound Road, Homestead, FL 33030, +1 305.248.8741, www.alabamajacks.com | Hours Daily 11am–6:30pm | Tip Another great biker bar is Scully's Tavern (9809 SW 72nd St) in Miami. Although Scully's doesn't have Alabama Jack's famous fritters, the atmosphere is on par and the food isn't too shabby either.

3 Amertec Building

Hialeah's abandoned alien

In 1967, architect Chayo Frank was asked by his father to design a building to house his architectural woodworking and store-fixture manufacturing business. The resulting cluster of organically shaped structures falls somewhere between the imaginary worlds of Dr. Seuss and Jules Verne. Either an urban eyesore or an architectural masterpiece, depending on your taste and perspective, the old Amertec building has unwittingly come to simultaneously represent the struggle of Miami's impoverished and the city's affinity for innovation and artistic self-expression.

Made possible through the use of sprayed concrete, Frank's vision of tubes, bars, and curves materialized into the explosion of contours, colors, and textures that still sits along an industrial stretch of road in Hialeah. The unconventional building might best be described as a beautiful mess: a bright orange two-story mollusk shell, decorated by a strip of bacon, forms the entry facade to what looks like a giant twisting vent hose with a one-story mushroom dome at its southeast corner.

Stricken with some of the highest crime rates in the country, Hialeah has been a community perpetually on the mend. Falling victim to the area's deterioration over the years, the building, once coated in pearlescent blues and oranges (to give the "exterior more of a lifelike quality," according to Frank), was painted completely white upon Amertec-Granada Inc's sale in 2002. A calcified mummy of the amorphous blob – empty and abandoned – was all that remained on W 21st Street until a produce company took it over, repainted it, and turned it into a storage facility.

Sandwiched between faded warehouse facades, the green tubes, orange spirals, and beige domes are as hard to make any sense of today as they were when first constructed; not only on the streets of Hialeah nestled under the Metrorail, but anywhere on planet Earth.

Address 149 W 21 Street, Hialeah, FL 33010 | Tip Check out the fledgling Leah Arts District in Hialeah (from E 9th St to E 17th St, and E 10th Ave to the railroad tracks). This area features warehouse facades adorned in graffiti like its counterpart in Wynwood.

4 Ancient Spanish Monastery
Medieval Spain in Miami

Just off the Intercoastal Waterway, across the street from a modest apartment complex in North Miami Beach, sits a religious fortress nearly 800 years older than the city itself. Built in A.D. 1141 in Sacramenia, Spain, the Ancient Spanish Monastery is now tucked away on a sleepy stretch of Dixie Highway, a stone's throw from the ocean it had to cross to get here.

A gravel walkway leads visitors on a stroll through the Segovian iron gate, flush with palms, ferns, and other tropical flora. The well-kept geometric gardens are like a poor man's Versailles, featuring plush squares of grass delicately bordered by flowering shrubs. These gardens are the grand entrance into cavernous, Romanesque hallways beneath the bell tower that lead into an earlier place and time.

Cistercian monks had been the cloisters' only inhabitants for nearly 700 years in Spain. In the early 19th century, the buildings were seized and sold off. Fast-forward to 1925, when William Randolph Hearst bought the structure, had it dismantled stone by stone, and had it all shipped to the United States in 11,000 hay-packed wooden crates. Hoof-and-mouth disease had become an epidemic in Segovia, so upon their arrival in America, the crates were quarantined and remained in storage for 26 years. Falling on hard times, Hearst auctioned off the displaced stones, which fell into the hands of two Ohio businessmen. They decided to rebuild the structure in Miami, finishing it in 1964.

A palpable quiet emanating from the courtyard, draped in the hanging fruits of a kigelia tree, lingers in the halls of the original cloisters. Small, ornate stained-glass windows featuring gold crosses embedded in a mosaic of purples, yellows, reds, and blues shimmer in a dark room above the flickering novena candles at the base of the four-foot Christ the King statue. Come for a day of peace among the ghosts of ancient Spanish monastics.

Address 16711 W Dixie Highway, North Miami Beach, FL 33160, +1 305.945.1461, www.spanishmonastery.com | **Hours** Mon–Sat 10am–4:30pm, Sun 11am–4:30pm; call ahead in case of special closures | **Tip** Though the Ancient Spanish Monastery dates from the 12th century, it has only been in Miami since the 1960s. The city's oldest church is the beautiful Gesu Church (118 NE 2nd St, Miami), constructed in 1896.

5   Anne's Beach

Florida's best rest stop

A drive through the Keys, as beautiful as the surroundings are, can become monotonous. Roadside souvenir shops, lime-colored storefronts, and motels blur into one another along the 100-mile journey down US-1 from Key Largo to Key West. God forbid there happens to be traffic. If you are stuck, your car will idle over some of the country's most pristine waters. Looking out to sea, you'll see mangrove islands sprouting randomly from beneath the surface, and the temptation to jump out of your car and meander up to them in crystal clear shin-deep water is almost irresistible. Fortunately, there's a parking lot at mile marker 73.5 on the east side of Overseas Highway that allows you to do just that. Here you'll discover a small picturesque stretch of sand at the southern tip of Lower Matecumbe that beckons you to indulge.

Named after Anne Eaton, an environmentalist committed to preserving the natural beauty of this slice of subtropical heaven in Islamorada, Anne's Beach, with its pavilions and boardwalk, offers unparalleled views. Despite being stricken with polio when she was 24 years old and left bound to a wheelchair, Eaton spent much of her life making a global effort as a conservationist.

Today, the massive expanse of uninterrupted blue water reaches past the horizon, blending into the sky. Even at high tide, you can wade out a few hundred feet without the water rising above your knees. At low tide, the sand crabs come out of their burrows and scurry among the tide pools, and a vast field of shells is exposed, offering one of the best beachcombing spots in all of the Keys.

You won't find a gas station at this rest stop, but you will be able to refuel your body and mind, which is probably just as Eaton intended it. You can park your car, kick your shoes off, and sprint into the warm shallow waters – the ones you've been itching to frolic in for the past 50 miles.

Address Mile Marker 73.5, Lower Matecumbe, Islamorada, FL 33036, +1 305.664.6400 |
Tip If you're leisurely making your way down to Key West, there are many interesting roadside
stops along the way. The Turtle Hospital (2396 Overseas Hwy) offers a touching opportunity
to learn about and get up close and personal with injured and rehabilitated sea turtles.

6__Area 31

Happy hour with a view

At around five o'clock, when the workday is done, half-off drafts and BOGO deals run wild at every watering hole in Miami-Dade County. But perched 16 stories above the boozy melee below is where you'll find the happiest of all happy hours, in the Epic Hotel's bar/restaurant, Area 31.

The futuristic bar, whose bottles glow in front of an illuminated glass wall, welcomes you to Area 31's interior, fit with sleek, white leather seats and minimalist wood tables. Head bartender Dean Feddaoui and his team toil away, pouring some of the best cocktails in Downtown, featuring modern interpretations of traditional classics like the Royal Collins, with acai liqueur, local honey, lemon, egg whites, lavender bitters, and tonic. For something more adventurous, try one of Feddaoui's newfangled creations like the Simple Truth, with Wild Turkey rye, Luxardo maraschino, Aztec chocolate bitters, and lemon peel.

But the real draw is the dramatic view from the terrace. Just like its elevation, Area 31 gracefully straddles the line between high-society grandiloquence and down-to-earth sensibilities. Amid the towering skyscrapers of ritzy Downtown, with the giant ring in between the two towers of 500 Brickell looming overhead, a mixed crowd of locals and visitors mingles and imbibes. The happy-hour prices are as stellar as the location. From 5pm to 8pm during the week and from 5pm to midnight on Fridays, cocktails are served on the cheap in one of the city's most expensive neighborhoods. Premium wells, house wine, beer, and champagne all cost seven bucks. There's a $7 bar menu too, with cosmopolitan finger foods like ceviche tostadas and truffle fries.

As the sun begins to set, *Miami Vice* is revived on the terrace, with men sporting aviators and untucked pastel button-downs, and women wearing short, tight black dresses. Stiff as the drinks may be, Miami's illuminated skyline is the perfect chaser.

Address Epic Hotel, 70 Biscayne Boulevard Way, 16th Floor, Miami, FL 33131,
+1 305.424.5234, www.area31restaurant.com | **Hours** Happy Hour: Mon–Thu 5pm–8pm,
Fri 5pm–midnight | **Tip** Another restaurant with a view is Tuyo (415 NE 2nd Ave), also in
Downtown. Tuyo is affiliated with the Miami-Dade College Culinary Institute, and features
high-end contemporary American fare with an incredible view of the Freedom Tower.

7 __ Atlantis Condominiums

Miami Vice lives on

With the drug trade in full swing, the television crime drama *Miami Vice* was the perfect medium to show the world what Miami had become since its formative years as a sleepy beach town. For five seasons, Crockett and Tubbs policed the city's mean streets and waters during the eighties. And in the opening credits of every episode stood this rare architectural bird that gets lost today among the glass and concrete wilderness on Brickell Avenue.

Completed in 1982, the Atlantis Condominiums personify the archetypical building style of Miami's salad days. Much like a pubescent teen, the city experienced unpleasant growing pains throughout the latter part of the 20th century. With a deeper voice and taller stature came drastic mood swings and regular distress. Drug violence was rampant, with mall shootings and drive-bys making local headlines almost every night. Throngs of Cuban refugees, many of whom had been prisoners under Fidel Castro, flooded makeshift camps underneath the highways. The old Miamians were moving up the coast, leaving behind a city they'd come to see as hopeless.

Despite all the adversity that consumed Miami, so too did a zeal to create a better future, at least aesthetically. When *Miami Vice* was at its peak, the city had become a pretty face with loose moral foundations. High-rises, many founded on dirty money, started growing explosively across town. The architecture firm Arquitectonica spearheaded the shift toward relative decency, with nearly 30 of its bold buildings still accenting the jagged skyline from the mainland to Miami Beach.

In *Miami Vice*, this achromatic giant is seen with a hollow square palm court cut out of the middle, complete with its iconic red spiral staircase cranked through it like a corkscrew. More than 30 years later, the Atlantis Condominiums are still as slick and open-shirted as the iconic cops played by Don Johnson and Philip Michael Thomas.

Address 2025 Brickell Avenue, Miami, FL 33129 | Tip Drive around and look at the old houses on the north side of Brickell by Atlantis Condominiums. Many are built atop elevated coral shelves, a reminder that the waters of Biscayne Bay once extended much farther inland.

8   Bahia Honda

Sleep with the fishes

In Florida, camping is a sticky, mosquito-laden experience. Stagnant 80-degree nights, only made hotter by the intense burn of citronella candles, are what greet the South Floridian camper most of the year. Many campgrounds in the urban sprawl are within earshot of the nearest thoroughfare, so even seclusion is hard to come by when pitching a tent in the "wilderness." But less than an hour away from Key West, one of the most beautiful, remote camping spots in South Florida awaits you, at Bahia Honda.

Nearly all of South Florida's waterfront land is overdeveloped. Condominiums, mansions, hotels, and restaurants dominate the shoreline from Palm Beach to Miami. Sure, there are some parks, but they are perpetually filled with humanity. The average public green space has a handful of picnic pavilions, the stray charcoal grill, weathered dunes, and a beach that's been dredged many times over. On the other hand, there's Bahia Honda, the sparkling emerald of the Keys; it's not only one of the few undisturbed beachfronts in the region, but also one of the only beaches on which you can spend the night.

For the outdoorsy types, there are traditional campgrounds perfect for setting up a tent and roughing it for a few days. But for those not as inclined to forgo creature comforts, there are six cabins situated along a cove on the southern half of the Key. For less than $200 a night, you can drive your car into the carport and stay in your own beach house, complete with central air-conditioning, hot water, bedrooms (with beds!), and bathrooms (with toilets!). From this convenient home base, you can explore the island's pristine beaches and diverse flora and fauna. If you're lucky, you'll even catch a glimpse of the magnificent Miami blue butterfly.

The only hitch is that the cabins are in such high demand they're generally booked at least one year in advance; sometimes paradise requires a little planning.

Address 36850 Overseas Highway, Big Pine Key, FL 33043, +1 305.872.3210, www.bahiahondapark.com | Hours Daily 8am–sunset | Tip Forty minutes west of the park, on Big Pine Key, sits an unusual drinking establishment for locals and tourists alike. From the outside, No Name Pub (30813 Watson Blvd) looks like a standard bar, but its interior is completely blanketed in dollar bills, either stuck to or hanging from all the walls and ceilings.

9__Bay of Pigs Museum
A tragedy remembered

Nearly all of Miami's Cuban residents came to Florida when dictator Fidel Castro, who assumed power in Cuba in 1959, squeezed them out. Cuba's wealthiest were the first to arrive, their assets having been seized, their relatives jailed. In 1960, the Brigada Asalto 2506 was formed, a group of Cuban exiles in Miami whose goal was to overthrow Castro with assistance from the CIA. A block south of Calle Ocho in Little Havana, on Ninth Street, the legend and legacy of Brigade 2506 lives on.

The soldiers that comprised the troop were not highly specialized fighters but a representative cross-section of the Cuban population: farmers, lawyers, priests, doctors, and even defectors from Castro's revolutionary army. Together, they prepared to overthrow the dictator and his stifling oppression.

After nine months of training, it was finally "go" time for this group of 430 men. The brigade, launched from Guatemala, landed on the shores of Playa Giron in the Bay of Pigs on April 17, 1961. The objective of the invasion was to complete a coup d'état by overwhelming the Cuban militia with soldiers on the ground and airstrikes from above. The CIA was supposed to provide air support upon the brigade's landing, but President Kennedy did not give final approval, leaving the small band to fend for themselves as they stormed the beach.

A foreign-policy disaster for the United States ended up being a tragedy for Brigade 2506. At the Bay of Pigs museum, the walls are covered from floor to ceiling in photographs commemorating the individual soldiers – the overwhelming majority of whom were either killed or captured – who served in this futile battle. The museum was established in 2005 by a few of its surviving members as an homage to their brave effort to take back their native Cuba; Brigada Asalto 2506's official motto: "We will never abandon our homeland."

ANTONINO DIAZ POU
11 Diciembre 1934 + 6 Diciembre 1961

Joven de vida ejemplar, estudioso y trabajador que
ofrendó su vida por el ideal de una patria justa, próspera y solidaria
para todos los cubanos, sin distinción de raza, género o creencias.
Las generaciones futuras de santacruceños deben conocer su vida para
forjar una sociedad en la que el respeto a la opinión ajena prevalezca
sobre el odio y la intolerancia que tanto sufrimiento han traído a
la nación cubana.

2-506

Address 1821 SW 9th Street, Miami, FL 33135, +1 305.649.4719, www.bayofpigs2506.com | **Hours** Mon–Fri 9am–4pm, Sat 10am–4pm | **Tip** Check out the Bay of Pigs monument on Calle Ocho at the corner of SW 8th Street and SW 13th Avenue. The eternal flame still burns atop the black granite pillar, dedicated to those who lost their lives in the battle.

10__Betsy the Giant Lobster

If only she was on the menu ...

At the intersection of Overseas Highway and Gimpy Gulch Drive, near mile marker 87, a 30-foot-tall, 40-foot-long, anatomically correct spiny crustacean is an incontrovertible reminder that you are most definitely in the Florida Keys.

Betsy the lobster was conceived in the 1980s by sculptor Richard Blaze of Marathon, who spent five years constructing and perfecting her for a company that would ultimately go out of business just before Betsy's completion. Essentially born an orphan, Betsy was bought, or adopted, by Tom Vellanti for the front of Treasure Village, an old Islamorada landmark that was a shopping center for independent merchants and craftspeople. When Treasure Village was turned into a Montessori school in 2006, Betsy was again homeless. She was disassembled and put on eBay in the hopes of being auctioned off, but there were no takers. In 2009, the owners of the Rain Barrel, an artists' community and marketplace, bought Betsy and put her back on display, greeting passersby like she was made to do.

And since 2009, Betsy has stayed put, right across the street from her old home at Treasure Village. Betsy's whiplike antennules and spiny, jagged legs may startle those who aren't expecting her – the details are too real. Her carapace – with intricate designs in different shades of red, brown, and white – glistens under the Keys' bright sun. Her antennae stretch more than 30 feet from her black, tranquil eyes to her brilliant, fanned tail.

Smaller and a little less juicy than their famous cousins to the north, lobsters in the Keys can only be caught and sold during certain times of the year. If you've never been a part of lobster season in Florida, take advantage of it. Divers can grab their dinner straight from the sea during spiny lobster season, from August 6 to March 31 or amid the bedlam of the two-day "mini season" on the last Wednesday and Thursday in July.

Address 86700 Overseas Highway, Islamorada, 33036, +1 305.852.3084 | Tip Head south on Overseas Hwy to the end of Islamorada and stop off at Bud N' Mary's Marina (79851 Overseas Hwy). Since 1944, the marina has been the hub of sport fishing in the Keys. Charter a boat and experience firsthand the incredible fishing the area has to offer.

11 Big Cypress Gallery
Ansel Adams of the Everglades

Right off the old Tamiami Trail, in Collier County, is an old wooden house with flags fluttering in the wind near its entrance. Inside, crystal-clear monochromatic photographs, many blown up to over five feet in width or height, hang on the walls as portals into Florida's rugged, enchanting Everglades. Clyde Butcher has carved himself a niche as the country's premier photographer of Florida's natural wonders. Sixty miles west of Downtown Miami, Butcher's gallery is in the middle of it all, in the middle of nowhere.

Butcher began his venture into photography when he attended an Ansel Adams exhibit at Yellowstone in the 1960s. He was so inspired by Adams's ability to capture landscapes in black-and-white that he decided to take a crack at it himself. Tremendous success accompanied Butcher in the years that followed. He established his own multimillion-dollar photography business, selling his work to major department stores like J.C. Penney and Sears. However, the stress of owning such a huge company with more than 200 employees became too much of a burden for Butcher. He sold the business in 1977, bought a sailboat, and hauled it to Florida to start his next chapter.

Tragedy struck in 1986, when his son was killed by a drunk driver, and Butcher retreated to the wilderness of the Big Cypress National Preserve to find solace. There he discovered a huge chunk of natural, untouched beauty. One and a half million acres of saw-grass prairie, wetlands, pinelands, and hardwood hammocks cover the central portion of Florida's southern half. Spanish moss drips from the limbs of old-growth oaks. Ferns blanket fallen tree trunks floating in the marshy slough. Cattails sprout out of this six-mile-wide "river of grass," while the sporadic alligator lifts its snout from under the surface. The Everglades explode with life, and renowned photographer Clyde Butcher captures its essence better than anyone.

Address 52388 Tamiami Trail E, Ochopee, FL 34141, +1 239.695.2428, www.clydebutcher.com | **Hours** Daily 10am–5pm | **Tip** Visit Butcher's other gallery and darkroom in Venice (237 Warfield Ave), a little over two hours northwest of the Big Cypress Gallery.

12 Bill Baggs Cape Florida State Park

Solitude by the city

Above all else, Miami is defined by its world-class beaches. The beauty of their clean, warm waters and untouched sands lured people to Florida in droves during the forties and fifties. In the eighties, they welcomed Latino immigrants to America just as the Statue of Liberty greeted European immigrants at the turn of the 20th century. Today, they're where tourists go to relax and locals go to catch their breath.

Over Rickenbacker Causeway, through Virginia Key, and down Crandon Boulevard lies Bill Baggs State Park, at the southern tip of Key Biscayne. Only a 20-minute drive from downtown, the park feels completely detached from Miami's pulsing city center. Bill Baggs' human traffic is just a fraction of that on South Beach; if it's peace and nature you're seeking, there is no better stretch of shoreline.

You won't find any umbrellas and chaise lounges awaiting you at the end of the boardwalk that leads to the beach – just soft, white sands that pave the way to the emerald waters advancing and retreating in the distance. Clusters of sea oats punctuate the dunes, while rich, green mangroves and sea grapes frame the sands below, offering a uniquely Floridian beauty in its contrast.

If you get there early enough, you'll see the sun peek its head out from under the Atlantic to the east, and strike the bright white facade of Cape Florida's lighthouse, Miami-Dade County's oldest standing structure. If you stick around all day (an easy thing to do), you'll catch the sun fizzle into Biscayne Bay to the west, dotted by Miami's skyline.

Bill Baggs is more than just a picturesque beach. It's a representation of how the city pauses to recharge and collect itself. Miami may inhale through South Beach, Downtown, and the Port, but it exhales through Bill Baggs.

Address 1200 Crandon Boulevard, Key Biscayne, FL 33149, +1 305.361.5811, www.floridastateparks.org/capeflorida | Hours Daily 8am–sundown | Tip Up the road from Bill Baggs is the Oasis (19 Harbor Dr), an unassuming Key Biscayne eatery that offers basic but delicious Cuban food.

13__Black Point Marina

Sea cow sanctuary

In the winter months, manatees, the large mild-mannered sea mammals of South Florida, flock en masse to the waters of Black Point Marina. When the temperature dips, these creatures congregate here to wallow in the warmest waters around. Biscayne Bay and the Atlantic Ocean pale in comparison to Black Point Marina, which has the hot "Jacuzzi" temperatures that sea cows desperately seek when fleeing the subtle chill of the region's winter waters.

What makes Black Point so unusually warm is a combination of the heat generated by boats traversing the marina and the runoff from the water treatment facility just upstream. This happy accident of converging nature and industry provides ideal conditions for a merry group of manatees. Boats are prohibited from entering the waters beyond the marina, as their propellers have become notorious for maiming or killing these lumbering gentle giants, too slow to avoid the sharp, whirring blades. If you manage to get close to one of the manatees, scars and mangled tails from past encounters will likely be visible.

Although the manatee is on the verge of extinction, many of these half-ton herbivores can still be seen in the wild in the shallow depths of Black Point. Notoriously lethargic, manatees may rest idly in the same spot for upwards of an hour, alerting you to their presence with an audible puff as they surface for air. Fortunately for onlookers, Black Point's relative isolation from watercraft and sea predators offers a fantastic nursery for manatees and their young. If the stars align, you may be lucky enough to see a mother and her calf, who will remain by her side for the first two years of its life.

The manatees of Black Point appear like floating potatoes, bobbing up and down in the distance. If they venture close enough to shore, their small whiskered faces come into view as they enjoy the sun's warm rays bouncing off their backs.

Address 24775 SW 87th Avenue, Homestead, FL 33032, +1 305.258.4092, www.miamidade.gov/parks/black-point-marina | Hours Open 24 hours | Tip Grab a bite to eat at the Black Point Ocean Grill, located at the northeast corner of the marina. Bring your fresh catch here after a day of fishing and the kitchen staff will cook it for you any way you like.

14_ Blue Hole

Freshwater oasis in a saltwater desert

The topography of the Florida Keys is unlike anywhere else in the country, let alone the state. On land, Florida hollies and their bright red berries line the streets of Overseas Highway between the peeling bark of gumbo-limbo trees and beneath the shade of scraggly Jamaican dogwoods. Driving over the water, turquoise and emerald is all you see in every direction. The waters surrounding the roads and bridges are so shallow, you can walk for hundreds of yards without getting your knees wet. It's apparent that the Keys were birthed from the ocean on the Florida Reef, but a small oasis in the middle of Big Pine Key indicates there's more to these rocky islands than meets the eye.

The Blue Hole is the only source of fresh water in the Keys, but it isn't naturally occurring. At the turn of the century, Henry Flagler, industrialist and founder of the Florida East Coast Railway, was building a railroad that stretched from Florida's mainland to Key West. During the process, limestone and other rocks were extracted for road fills. More than a century later, one particular rock quarry on Big Pine Key filled up with rainwater.

Structurally sustained by a barrier of salt water that flows underneath the fresh water, the Blue Hole has become a haven for a wide range of flora and fauna. The Key deer that populate Big Pine Key come here to quench their thirst. Birds commonly found in the Everglades, like anhingas and great blue herons, are also in residence here. Even a couple of alligators prowl the waters. The scenery is breathtaking and unique for the Keys. Instead of palm trees, there are the slash pines that typically populate the marshy regions of Florida.

The Blue Hole offers a shining example of nature gracefully co-opting a human endeavor. For an up-close view of the local wildlife and vegetation, there's a short, easy nature trail that runs the park's perimeter.

Address Key Deer Boulevard, Big Pine Key, FL 33043, +1 305.872.0074 | Hours Daily sunrise to sunset | Tip For those who want to get up-close and personal with South Florida's rich biosphere, they can "Slog the Slough" in Everglades National Park. Walk waist-deep through slow-moving waters with a guide and experience the interiors of the Everglades' many Cypress Domes, whose wildlife is very similar to that of the Blue Hole. Not for the faint of heart.

15 Boca Chita Key

Paradise found

Eleven miles east of Homestead is a paradise nearly indistinguishable from the beaches of Fiji and Bora Bora. As you cruise toward the Ragged Keys, your boat bouncing over every swell, a blurred line on the horizon comes into focus; a long stretch of islands appears, seemingly out of nowhere. Fast approaching land, you'll spot a 20-foot lighthouse, the de facto "Welcome to Boca Chita Key" sign. In Biscayne National Park, on this very special island, the public is welcome to an untouched delight, which anyone with a boat can enjoy. Tie up the line in the cove on Boca Chita's northwest corner, walk through the patches of pricklers and rough grass, and lay claim to your own secluded beach.

A small strip of sand is exposed on dry land, but the sea is so shallow you can walk knee-deep through the water to a number of the smaller surrounding islands. The sand underfoot is soft and grooved, indicative of minimal to no animal activity. Mangrove shoots, soft but spiny, stick out of the glassy water like stalagmites in a dank cavern. Thousands of large, intact seashells carpet the sandy bottom, begging to be plucked up and saved as mementos.

The water's color morphs with the depth of the seafloor. At its shallowest it looks perfectly clear, as if you're peering through a window into submerged cities of coral polyps populated by schools of small minnows. As you wade a little deeper, the water turns a pale turquoise, and at its deepest, takes on a majestic shade of blue green, illuminated by the midday sun.

Live the day like Tom Hanks in *Castaway*, but without the struggle. The island's unkempt beaches are your refuge. Seek shelter from the heat in a breezy, shaded alcove underneath the mangroves. Find sustenance in your cooler, filled with sandwiches and bottled water. Share the moment with your friends and family – or your Wilson volleyball.

Address Boca Chita Key is located 12 miles due south of Key Biscayne. | Tip For another unique experience of the bay, try nighttime paddleboarding at Miami Beach Paddleboard (1416 18th St). The underside of each board is fitted with powerful LED lights, which illuminate the dark waters, revealing the nocturnal activities in the sea beneath and around you.

16   Brickell Soccer Rooftop

Fútbol in the financial district

Over the past half century, Miami has seen the population of its skyline explode. Open space in Downtown is nearly impossible to come by, so vertical growth has increased to accommodate all those working and living off Brickell Avenue. Luckily for many, the recreation they seek is at the beach, easily accessed either via the Rickenbacker Causeway to Key Biscayne or across the MacArthur Causeway to Miami Beach. For those looking for more than the ocean breeze, there's an Astroturf oasis on the roof of a small office building at the mouth of the Miami River.

Encased in mesh walls, the soccer field stands alone, lost among the myriad of megastructures surrounding the pitch. The field and nets are smaller than regulation size, but the landscape they're situated in is larger than life. Incredible towering hotels, condos, and office buildings are the grounds' spectators. At the southern end of the field, a parking garage with a polka-dot color gradient lies flush with the goal line. High above its rainbow facade hovers the otherworldly halo of 500 Brickell. The large white circular perforation, hundreds of feet in the air, harnesses the sunlight and looks down on the field like a deity. At the northern end, the Miami River, flanked by skyscrapers, spills into Biscayne Bay.

The field is available to rent hourly for practice or organized matches throughout the week, and also hosts local leagues and offers soccer lessons to kids on Sundays.

In the midst of Miami's melting pot, it's only natural that the international game of soccer has bubbled over and found a home in Downtown's sweaty concrete jungle. Latin Americans constitute two-thirds of the city's population, and what's common among them is an undying passion for *fútbol*. Talk of Miami getting its own professional team has been in the air for some time, but hinges on the financing and construction of a major-league soccer stadium.

Address 444 Brickell Avenue, 2nd Floor, Miami, FL 33131, +1 305.967.3512, www.soccerooftop.com | Hours Mon–Fri 4pm–midnight, Fri–Sat 9am–midnight | Tip Head north on Miami Avenue to Fooq's (1035 N Miami Ave), a contemporary American restaurant with one of the best burgers in town. Short rib, skirt steak, and brisket comprise this patty, topped with a layer of melted Jarlsberg and served on a toasted, buttered brioche.

17 — The Calle Ocho Walk of Fame

Looking down at the stars

Strolling along Calle Ocho in Little Havana – the most celebrated stretch of road in the most lionized Latin-American neighborhood in the country – gaze down and you'll notice a series of stars embedded in the cement, much like those famously found on Hollywood Boulevard. A testament to the influence and presence of Cuban and Latino culture in Miami, the Calle Ocho Walk of Fame pays well-deserved homage to some of the most prominent Latino figures in modern society, ensuring they will never be forgotten.

Plenty of debate once surrounded the stars that have lined this avenue for nearly 30 years. The matter of who should merit a place on the Walk of Fame was deeply vetted in the beginning. Should the honorees only be of Cuban descent? Should they have direct ties to South Florida? A selection committee was formed and as time passed, the arguments slowly faded. Today any distinguished Latino can be considered for inclusion.

Superstar musician and Miami's unofficial ambassador, Gloria Estefan, earned her star in 1989. Roberto Duran, the notorious Panamanian boxer, also has a star on the walk. Celia Cruz, the queen of salsa, received the inaugural star in 1988. Although she passed away in 2003, Cruz's presence and legacy is still felt throughout Little Havana, where her face and song lyrics are muralized on walls.

Latin – predominantly Cuban – culture enraptures the senses on Calle Ocho. Taste its savory empanadas, smell its rich cigar smoke wafting from the many factories, hear its pounding batá drums on the street corners, feel its heat and humidity in the air of Little Havana, and see its stars beneath your feet. In a neighborhood that's witnessed extraordinary change over the past few decades, the permanence of the Walk of Fame is a point of pride.

Address South side of Calle Ocho, from SW 17th Ave to SW 13th Ave, Miami, FL 33135 | **Tip** Before your star walk, get a Cuban treat at the window of Exquisito Restaurant (1510 SW 8th St). Seventy-five cents is about the best deal you'll find for a cortadito, a shot of sweet Cuban espresso.

18 __ Cat Man

Not a dog-and-pony show

"Cat show for cat people! Five minutes! Don't be late, we are never on time!" Dominique LeFort announces with a wink to chortling visitors strolling the docks. Cats cannot be trained, so goes conventional wisdom. Or at least they can't be trained by anyone but Dominique. Dominique and his house cats, as silly as they are impressive, have traveled all over the country, performing in most every major American city. Fortunately for Floridians, they've made Key West their home.

Every evening at dusk by the docks near Mallory Square, the clever felines are unveiled. Dominique goads Chopin, the "smart one," to climb the rope up to his pedestal. "Take your time, hurry up," he chirps as Chopin hesitates to leap. Mandarine, the orange tabby, begins to make a move across a tightrope. "Stay where you are, do what you want!" Dominique shouts as he lights his ring of fire. One by one, his cats leap through the hoop on a high wire to the oohs and aahs of the gathered crowd.

Dominique has been a street performer for most of his adult life. He got his start as an aspiring entertainer at the Lecoq school, studying improvisation, modern dance, and miming. He became a clown under the stage name Rou Dou Dou, performing his one-hour, one-man show everywhere from Las Vegas to Montreal. It was during this time that – inspired by his daughter's kitten, Chaton – Dominique decided to incorporate cats into his act, and the legend of the Cat Man was born soon after.

Since 1981, Dominique and his crew of kitties have been entertaining the masses here at Key West Harbor. Against the backdrop of a setting sun, the frizzy-haired Frenchman, still sporting his circa-1980s mullet, struts around his impromptu circus ring like a wildly eccentric ringmaster, bantering with the audience, himself, and the sky above, as his cats put on a spectacle that rivals anything you'll see under the Big Top.

Address The docks behind the Westin Hotel, located at 245 Front Street, Key West, FL 33040, +1 305.304.7764, www.catmankeywest.com | Hours Daily at sunset | Tip Mallory Square comes alive for the nightly sunset festival. Street performers fill the plaza. You'll find unusual characters like Big Bird walking around taking pictures for a dollar, a bagpiper playing native Scottish songs, and a man painted like a statue, holding a ball with an eager golden retriever at his feet.

19___Cauley Square

All aboard the kitsch caboose

In 1903, Lyman Gould operated a siding – a railroad junction that changes direction – on the Florida East Coast Railway in southern Dade County. This siding opened the proverbial floodgates for farmers of the Redlands, who finally had an efficient way to distribute their produce throughout the state, thanks to the recent extension of the rail line. The village soon attracted settlers, and into the 1920s, Cauley Square, named after Redlands farmer William Cauley, gained a reputation as a boisterous hub of mischief.

When the Great Hurricane of 1926 nearly destroyed the area, the community was abandoned and left to decay for more than 20 years. It was slated for demolition, when, in 1949, Mary Anne Ballard came to its rescue and purchased the 20-acre property. Ballard singlehandedly transformed Cauley Square from a rotting railroad settlement into a charming restoration of an old Florida town. Gone were the packinghouses, saloons, and bordellos that once populated this run-of-the-mill whistle stop. In their place were highlights of turn-of-the-century America: open plazas with rustic fountains, quirky craft stores, and a teahouse.

Cauley Square's old-time kitsch is a welcome break from Miami's urban sprawl. Filled with independent boutiques and shops, it's easy to while away an afternoon here. Buy authentic Haitian crafts at Island Colors or enjoy a glass of pinot while you take in some live music at the Village Chalet. No visit is complete without a stop at the Tea Room, filled with decorative butterflies, lace tablecloths, and stained-glass lamps.

Out of the dust of brothels and watering holes, the charm of this "preserved" village seems untouched almost a century later. Cauley Square is the old Southern belle of Miami, sitting in her rocking chair wearing a whalebone corset and long dress, sipping a mint julep on the front porch in the dead of summer.

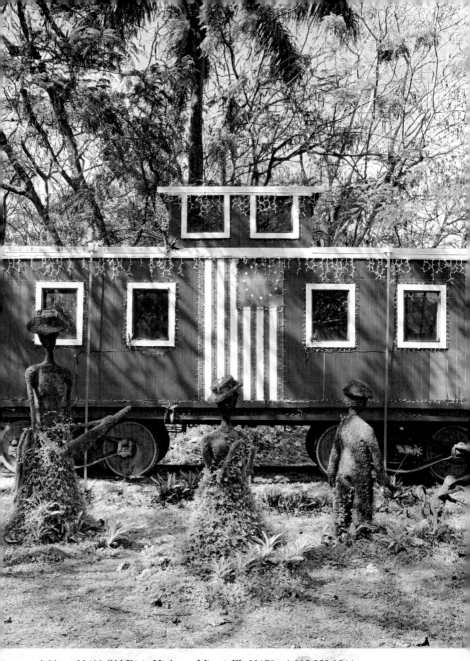

Address 22400 Old Dixie Highway, Miami, FL 33170, +1 305.258.0044,
www.cauleysquare.com | **Hours** Tue–Sun 11am–5pm | **Tip** On the way back to
Downtown, stop off at legendary rib joint Shorty's BBQ (9200 South Dixie Hwy).
Old-school communal wooden tables fill the log cabin, which was rebuilt after
burning down in 1972. The beef ribs are tremendous. Bring a change of clothes.

20__CIFO Tile Facade

Downtown's bamboo forest

In a field of parking lots and nightclubs, near one of the country's roughest neighborhoods in Overtown, a beautiful bamboo forest has made its home on the exterior of a contemporary art gallery. More than a million tiny tiles in 100-plus colors – an eclectic mosaic of oranges, greens, blues, and browns – appear like the pixels of a digital photograph when viewed up close. But with every step away from the wall, a lush jungle landscape filled with bamboo stalks and dripping vines begins to take shape.

Miami is making a name for itself by finding beauty in places where anything but bleakness was once tough to come by, and the shimmering tile exterior of CIFO is a sign of the times. For years, this neighborhood was gradually decaying into irrelevancy, stricken with poverty, crime, and urban blight. The area's art-inspired makeover began in 1990, with the installation of Oldenburg and van Bruggen's *Dropped Bowl* outside Government Center, and soon spread throughout Downtown and into Wynwood and Hialeah.

The concept of the gallery itself echoes this evolution. Ella Fontanals-Cisneros, the founder of CIFO, established her foundation in 2002 in order to "support artists who are exploring new directions in contemporary art." Expect the unexpected inside: an abstract exhibition dangling from the ceilings; a web of fluorescent lights hanging on the walls; a broken mirror re-formed into a portrait; and arrows on the floor beneath your feet pointing you toward major world cities.

CIFO's exterior, however, is undoubtedly what draws people to its doors. In the span of ten months, architect Rene Gonzalez and his team laid the tiles individually by hand, ready in time to show off to the world for Art Basel in 2005. The 20-foot-tall forest wall blends with the real, living bamboo in the courtyard, creating a graceful blend of art and life.

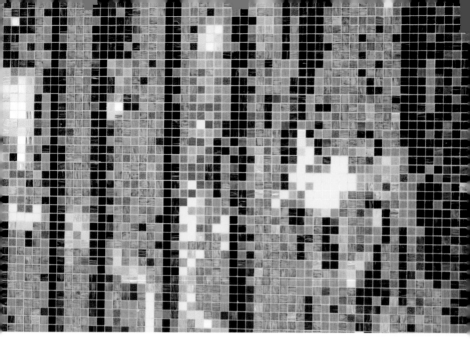

Address 1018 N Miami Avenue, Miami, FL 33136, +1 305.455.3333, www.cifo.org | **Hours** Thu–Fri 12pm–6pm, Sat–Sun 10am–4pm | **Tip** CIFO is in the middle of Downtown's burgeoning bar and nightclub district. Club hop and bar crawl into the wee hours of the morning from Club Space (light shows with a live DJ playing trance and house music; 34 NE 11th St) to the Corner (low-key tavern serving creative cocktails to locals; 1035 N Miami Ave).

21__City Hall

Seaplanes and city managers

In the early days of Miami, Dinner Key, a small island in Biscayne Bay, was accessible only by boat. In 1914, the Army Corps of Engineers connected it to the mainland by filling in the surrounding waters to create a training field for the US Navy during World War I. In the 1930s and '40s, Pan American World Airways turned Dinner Key into its primary base of operations. The booming airline connected North and South America by way of its luxurious "Flying Clipper Ships," tremendous metallic propeller planes that would put today's international first class accommodations to shame.

Outfitted with full kitchens, "deluxe compartments," sleeping cabins, and dining rooms, the heavy round-bottomed aircrafts could take off from and land on the smooth waters of Biscayne Bay. The seaplanes' popularity was due in part to a lack of sufficient runways in South America and across the globe. During this time, aboard Pan Am's Dixie Clipper, Franklin D. Roosevelt stopped in Dinner Key en route to Morocco to meet with Winston Churchill at the Casablanca Conference in 1943.

As runways became more popular, it spelled the end of the flying boat. With Pan Am's last flight departing from Dinner Key in 1945, the city of Miami bought much of the land on Dinner Key and what had been the hub for the majority of the country's international flights.

Less than ten years after the purchase, the city also made a move to preserve the Art Deco Pan Am terminal by turning it into City Hall. The old seaplane hangars now house boats for the massive Dinner Key Marina complex. Boats are tied to slips where the old clippers used to taxi and take off. At the foot of a large cul-de-sac, the pearlescent City Hall can be blinding in the sunlight. In a classic Art Deco font, "Miami City Hall" broadcasts itself above the concrete awning. A nautical shade of blue accents the building, echoing the color of the Pan Am logo.

Address 3500 Pan American Drive, Miami, FL 33133, +1 305.250.5400 | Tip If all that aviation history gets you hungry, head over to LuLu (3105 Commodore Plaza), a tapas bar in the heart of Coconut Grove, just a few blocks away. Try a little bit of everything, because that's what tapas are for.

22 Clevelander at Marlins Park

Poolside in left field

Nowhere in the world except Miami can you find an outdoor, bumping discotheque – with a swimming pool! – inside a baseball stadium. At Marlins Park in Little Havana, South Beach's famous Clevelander hotel and nightclub has a satellite location right next to the visiting team's bullpen. Out in left field, with a so-so line of sight to the game, girls dance on pedestals while cocktails and beer are served hand over fist. Some clubgoers shimmy the night away to beats delivered by the in-house DJ. Others kick back in the pool – at least until a home-run ball splashes into the deep end, reminding them that just a few feet away, a major-league baseball game is being played.

Dwarfed by the dominance of basketball and football, baseball has always been Miami's neglected stepchild no matter how well the Marlins have performed. But just as South Beach had its renaissance, the Marlins are attempting theirs. Owner and successful art dealer Jeffrey Loria erected a lavish new stadium in 2012; temperature controlled and complete with retractable roof, it's a contemporary jewel in Little Havana.

This park is full of goodies. The backstops behind home plate are aquariums filled with live fish. Above the outfield, underneath the expansive windows that showcase Miami's Downtown skyline, is a giant Red Grooms sculpture with rows of flipping marlins, which activates whenever Miami hits a home run.

But the stadium's most special feature is without a doubt its Clevelander. On Saturdays, the ballpark club hosts Noche Caliente, a live salsa band that performs two hours before and after the game As the drinks flow from the first inning to the ninth, the proverbial sun is always shining on South Beach in left field, no matter how the Marlins fare.

Address 501 Marlins Way, Miami, FL 33125, +1 305.532.4006, www.miami.marlins.mlb.com/mia/ballpark/clevelander.jsp | Hours Open two hours before first pitch to two hours after the game is over; check the Marlins' website for the home game schedule. | Tip Once the Marlins' Clevelander closes up shop, continue the party at South Beach's famous original Clevelander (1020 Ocean Dr, Miami Beach).

23___Club Nautico

See Miami in its element

What the Seine is to Paris and Lake Michigan is to Chicago, Biscayne Bay is that and more to Miami. A shining example of a marine trade and tourism route, its warm, emerald waters beckon everybody within eyeshot to partake in its treasures. Among the best ways to turn the bay into your playground for a day is to make a quick stop at Club Nautico and choose from their wide variety of posh powerboats and yachts.

Club Nautico caters to both seasoned and green boaters. If you're experienced on the water and prefer something a little low key, consider a small motorboat. With a group of up to six people, you can ride the bay in a 20-foot Nautic Star; cruise up to the Chart House for lunch or zip around to view the pristine beaches of North Miami and the skyscrapers of Downtown. But if you want to do Miami the way P. Diddy does the French Riviera, splurge and charter a yacht complete with its own crew. Rent an 80-footer and stay a few nights on the high seas with a dozen friends, or if your wallet doesn't stretch that far, even one day in the lap of aquatic luxury makes for an unforgettable experience of the city and its surrounds.

Start the day early to catch the sunrise over the Atlantic. Speed eastward from the mainland and tie up the boat at Boca Chita (see p. 38), or anchor down at one of the Ragged Keys and discover your own personal paradise among the deserted white sands. Head north to Stiltsville (see p. 204) and idle through a maze of floating homes, each with its own eccentricities. Drop anchor in the middle of Biscayne Bay and snorkel its reef, exploring sea life ranging from small striped gobies to the endangered loggerhead turtle.

To catch a glimpse of Miami at its most spectacular, be sure to stay buoyant long enough to catch the sunset behind the skyline and causeways, lighting the city up in spectacular neon shades of pink, green, blue, and red.

Address 4000 Crandon Boulevard, Key Biscayne, FL 33149, +1 305.216.8879, www.clubnauticomiami.com | Hours Daily 8am–6pm | Tip Another fun way to get around Miami is by electric golf cart. Rent a DecoCart (www.decocarts.com), designed to minimize the struggle of navigating traffic and tight parking on South Beach.

24_Coconut Grove Playhouse

Part cinema, all history

Coconut Grove has always been a split community. On the east side, you'll find mansions, shopping malls, and high-end restaurants, shaded under giant ficus-tree canopies. To the west, poverty, drugs, and crime run rampant through dilapidated homes and housing projects. Since 1956, the now-shuttered Coconut Grove Playhouse on Charles Avenue has been a landmark in one of Miami's most tumultuous neighborhoods, straddling the line between destitution and excess.

In its heyday, the Playhouse saw its fair share of starpower. Bea Arthur performed here long before portraying a Miami native enjoying her sunset years in *The Golden Girls*. George C. Scott and Denzel Washington are also alums. Playwright Tennessee Williams premiered some of his greatest works on the Coconut Grove stage, and mounted a revival of *A Streetcar Named Desire*. After 50 years as the epicenter of the city's thriving theater scene, the Playhouse was boarded up in 2006 amid a few too many budget problems and bounced checks.

Today, although its interior remains closed, its exterior is being put to another entertaining use. The Austin-based Blue Starlite Mini Urban Drive-In has made a home for itself in the parking lot. The poignant nostalgia of old-time drive-ins is accounted for here, from the concessions to the films themselves. Head to the refreshment stand and grab a bag of freshly popped popcorn and a glass-bottled soda to enjoy while watching a cinema classic like *The Wizard of Oz* or *The Breakfast Club*. The outdoor theater also offers a sophisticated twist on some movie-house staples: instead of coating your popcorn in a butter-ish topping for instance, opt for a luxurious truffle oil supplied by the adjacent Taurus Beer & Whisk(e)y House. S'mores, complete with a mini fire to toast the marshmallows and melt the chocolate over, are offered alongside everybody's favorites, Milk Duds and Raisinettes.

Address 3500 Main Highway, Miami, 33133, www.miamiurbandrivein.com | **Hours** Schedule varies, check website | **Tip** Before the movie starts, park your car in the lot and explore the rich history of Coconut Grove at the Barnacle State Park (3485 Main Hwy). The Barnacle, the oldest home in Miami, was built in 1891 and formerly owned by Ralph Middleton Munroe, one of Coconut Grove's pioneers.

25 __ Coppertone Girl
Moon over Miami

In concrete jungles around the world, city dwellers seek out sanctuaries where they can breathe in some fresh air and recharge. New Yorkers have Central Park, Parisians have the Seine River Basin, and Miamians have white-sand beaches, with their unmistakable aroma of suntan lotion: that unique scent salad of coconut, vanilla, and something vaguely resembling latex. The fragrance alone can transport any South Floridian to their mental beach, as can the little blonde girl who stands three stories tall on Biscayne Boulevard.

A few blocks south of the 79th Street Causeway, Miami's sunburned mascot is exposed on the side of a drab white office building. The giant bashful pigtailed child looks back in shock at the small brown Cocker Spaniel pulling on the bottom of her bathing suit, exposing her pale-skinned behind. Legend has it that the original model for the Coppertone girl is the granddaughter of old Coppertone owner Charles E. Clowe, but the sign's design was the brainchild of former Brown & Bigelow pinup artist Joyce Ballantyne.

Although Miami's oldest toddler has called the city home for her entire life, she's been moved around quite a bit since being conceived in 1959. Her first address was on the side of the old Parkleigh House, across the street from the Freedom Tower, greeting barges and cruise ships with the famous suntan lotion's old slogan, "Don't be a paleface. Use Coppertone," as they passed in and out of port. In 1995, after spending four years in a warehouse, she took up residence on the Concord Building on Flagler Street. Seventeen years later, the bare-bottomed tot was again relocated, this time to the MiMo District.

For almost a decade now, she and her pup have stood above the massive iconic yellow block letters at 7300 Biscayne Boulevard, an enduring piece of Americana that residents once lightheartedly referred to as the "moon over Miami."

Address 7300 Biscayne Boulevard, Miami, FL 33138 | Tip The Coppertone sign is in the heart of Miami's Modern Architecture District on Biscayne Boulevard (aka "MiMo on BiBo"). Peruse old motels like the nearby Vagabond, Saturn, and Seven Seas, which exemplify the city's take on "Googie" architecture.

26 Coral Castle

A fortress built to mend a broken heart

Somewhere between an alligator farm and a smattering of Confederate flags sits Coral Castle, the "Taj Mahal" of Homestead, a suburb just 30 miles south of Miami.

Edward "Ed" Leedskalnin, a native of Latvia, never got over his broken heart when his fiancée Agnes broke off their engagement just a day before the wedding. Devastated, he left home and wandered around North America, eventually settling in Florida City in the 1920s. He spent the next 30 years sculpting massive coral and limestone structures, creating what we now know as Coral Castle, a tribute to Agnes that she would never see.

Ed had no patience for neighbors or prying eyes, so when plans were made for a subdivision near the original home of his sculptures in 1936, he moved the many tons of stones in the middle of the night to their current location in Homestead. No one knows how he did it. The only thing Ed ever said on the matter was that he understood "the laws of weight and leverage." Theories abound, ranging from reverse magnetism to black magic.

Within the massive compound, Ed's fantasy of marriage and a family plays out in strange ways. In the dining room, he built a 5,000-pound heart-shaped "Feast of Love" table, which is adorned with Ed's original ixora plant centerpiece. In the Throne Room, visitors can try out the royal platforms he built for himself, Agnes, their child, and his mother-in-law. If you happen to have a misbehaving youngster along for the ride, visit the Repentance Corner, furnished with stocks – one for a child and a taller set for Agnes in case she became "sassy."

Situated across the street from a Subway and a Pizza Hut, Coral Castle could easily be confused with a mini golf course, and one might well drive right by. But those who do stop and wander in will find a truly bizarre homage to unrequited love, with a mystique that rivals that of the world's biggest ball of yarn.

Address 28655 S Dixie Highway, Homestead, FL 33033, +1 305.248.6345, www.coralcastle.com | Hours Sun–Thu 8am–6pm, Fri and Sat 8am–8pm | Tip Just north on US 1 lies Shiver's BBQ (28001 S Dixie Hwy), one of Miami's oldest and best barbeque joints. Order a plate of smoky sloppy ribs and you won't be able to stop until it's hard to move.

27 __ Crandon Park Zoo
Free-range peacocks and iguanas

On what was originally the largest coconut plantation in the country, Crandon Park was established in 1947, seven years after the Matheson Family donated in excess of 800 acres to Dade County for a public green space. A year after the park was built, a traveling circus rolled through town and went out of business, leaving one goat, two black bears, and three monkeys stranded. The animals were purchased for $270, and on the northern third of Key Biscayne, Miami's first zoo was born.

Crandon Park had become one of the nation's premier zoos by the mid-1960s, with more than a thousand animals representing upwards of 350 species, including rare Asian elephants, white tigers, and an Indian rhino. But upon facing the wrath of Hurricane Betsy in 1965, the zoo's days were soon numbered. More than 250 animals perished when the storm surge flooded the beachfront park, and talks about relocating the zoo to a safer location in South Miami began. Fifteen years later, the Crandon Park zoo was closed, and its remaining residents were moved to what would become Zoo Miami.

Although the zoo animals have left Key Biscayne, the grounds, just steps from one of the most tranquil beaches in South Florida, are still there. Instead of lions and tigers pacing captive within their cages, wild peacocks strut around freely, showing off their electric blue bodies and opulent feathers, conspicuously stalking visitors for food. Iguanas, relatives of the lizards that didn't make the move to the new zoo, have colonized what is now Crandon Park Gardens. Get close enough to one and watch it scurry over the barren walking paths once packed with Miami's children. Animal enclosures, still painted with tropical murals from decades ago, sit empty within mazes of palms and shrubs. The bars are gone, but the structures remain as an aide-mémoire to the days of yore.

Address 6747 Crandon Boulevard, Key Biscayne, FL 33149, +1 305.361.5421,
www.miamidade.gov/parks/crandon | Hours Daily sunrise–sunset | Tip See what's come
of the old Crandon Park Zoo at Zoo Miami (12400 SW 152 Street), located in South
Miami near Kendall. One of the only free-range zoos in the country, the exhibits here are
completely cageless.

28 __ Cuba Tobacco Cigar Co.

Up in smoke on Calle Ocho

Cutting through the air like a hot knife through butter, the smoldering cigars of Little Havana provide the aromatic essence of Cuba's splendor as well as its plight. It's an unmistakable redolence. As the infamous Marxist revolutionary Che Guevara once said, "A smoke in times of rest is a great companion to the solitary soldier." Along every block of the perpetually bustling Calle Ocho, Cuban Americans, squeezed out of their native country by an oppressive government, enjoy their stogies full of flavor and a slow-burning sorrow.

Cuba Tobacco Cigar Co. is run by one of the oldest cigar manufacturing families in Cuba. The Bello family's roots in tobacco can be traced back to the 19th century, when Don Bello, of the Canary Islands, left for Cuba in search of a better growing climate. In 1896, Bello established his first cigar factory, Tabacalera Las Villas. After Fidel Castro assumed power in Cuba in 1959, he demanded the surrender of all cigar factories to the government, or else the owners would be declared traitors to the revolution. Stripped of their business, the Bellos relocated to Miami and eventually set up shop on 8th Street.

From the street, the establishment appears as just another storefront catering to its Spanish-speaking clientele. Inside, the smell of fresh tobacco is almost blinding. The piquant perfume gives vibrancy to the walls stacked with cigar boxes from floor to ceiling. The Bello family makes and sells their hand-rolled cigars here, ranging in size from the shorter Belicoso to the longer Esplendido.

Up front, regulars swap stories with the shopkeeper. In the back, rows of *tabacaleras* (rollers), seated at their respective cubicles, quietly wrap cigars. For tourists, the thrill of smoking a cigar rolled right in front of them is a novelty never to be forgotten. For the natives of Little Havana, it's both a comforting and bitter reminder of the past.

Address 1528 SW 8th Street, Miami, FL 33135, +1 305.649.2717, www.cubatobaccocigarco.com | **Hours** Daily 10am–6pm | **Tip** Complement your cigar with a glass of whiskey from the historic Ball & Chain lounge (1513 SW 8th St) across the street.

29 Deering Estate

Poor man's Vizcaya

In Coconut Grove, James Deering's famous Villa Vizcaya (see p. 206), 43 acres of waterfront property centered around a 30,000-square-foot Mediterranean Revival mansion, stands as one of Miami's most popular landmarks. But just over 12 miles down Old Cutler Road, James's brother Charles also built himself an estate. Although more modest than his younger brother's (relatively speaking, that is), Charles's homestead is equally enchanting.

The Deering family owned the International Harvesting Company, a major manufacturer of agricultural machinery, which made north of $100 million in annual sales by 1910. In 1922, for less than $70,000, Charles Deering built his three-story stone home overlooking Biscayne Bay. Deering only lived five more years after its completion, but he specified in his will that the property should remain in the family until the last of his children had passed away. In 1984, his youngest daughter, Barbara, died and the estate was bought by the State of Florida for over $22 million.

The subtlety of the Charles Deering Estate in comparison to Villa Vizcaya can be appreciated from both the exterior grounds and within the main house. In the backyard, palms line both sides of a small cove tucked away from the bay. Inside, though now air-conditioned, you can imagine how the sea breeze must have once pushed its way through the windows just beneath the Cuban barrel-tile roof. One of the most interesting features is the prohibition-era wine cellar, which remains as it did in the 1920s, secured with a three-ton bank-vault door hidden behind a moveable bookcase. When a hurricane swept through Miami in 1945, the cellar was flooded and the vault door sealed shut. The combination had been lost and so it remained unopened until 1985, when a renowned safecracker was summoned to break in. More than 4,000 bottles of wine were discovered neatly stored on a series of wooden shelves.

Address 16701 SW 72nd Avenue, Miami, FL 33157, +1 305.235.1668, www.deeringestate.com | Hours Daily 10am–4pm | Tip Picnics are encouraged at the Deering Estate. Before heading over, drop by the Asia Market (9525 SW 160th St) for some lunch provisions to enjoy on the estate grounds.

30 Domino Park

Playing by the numbers

Amid Calle Ocho's shameless catcalls, honking car horns, and impromptu Cuban drum circles, the click-clacking of domino tiles and *abuelitos* (grandfathers), fueled by a few too many *café con leches* and shouting to the heavens, are the only things you'll hear under the gazebos of Maximo Gomez Park (known locally as Domino Park). Near the entrance to the park there's a notable mural by Oscar Thomas depicting presidents of the American nations that attended the first Summit of the Americas in Miami, in 1994.

Gomez, the park's namesake, is Cuba's George Washington: the man who fought Spain to gain independence. In the middle of a jungle of fedoras and guayaberas (pocketed white button-down shirts), the essence of Gomez's Cuba lives on through conversation and the shuffling of ivory tiles.

A game of straight dominos starts with all the tiles facedown on the table and randomly mixed up. Each player grabs a tile from the pile; the one who pulls the domino with the highest denomination plays first, and then the tiles are reshuffled. Each player draws seven tiles, leaving the remaining dominos off to the side. The object is to empty your rack by laying dominos end to end on the table, where only matching numbers can touch.

Rain or shine, Domino Park is always alive with good-natured banter and competition. The ribbing ranges from giving a fellow player a hard time for moving too slowly to pointing out the rather large girth of his wife. Smiles are as common as a hollered *"Oyé, chico!"* Like mahjongg and shuffleboard, a game of dominos tends to belong to those in their sunset years. For many in Little Havana, the park is like an open-access recreation room at a Latino retirement home. In addition to its entertainment value, dominos are a good way to stay mentally sharp and a reason to get out of the house and socialize. If an idle mind is the devil's playground, at Domino Park, the angels preside.

Address 801 SW 15th Avenue, Miami, FL 33135, +1 305.859.2717 | Hours Daily 8am–6pm | Tip Catch an indie flick at the historic Tower Theater (1508 SW 8th St).

31 El-Carajo

Stop for the gas, stay for the food, take home the wine

Despite the maniacal drivers of Dade County, traveling by car is generally the safest and most efficient mode of transport. Public transit is too hit-or-miss and walking is almost unheard of – and often life-threatening. The downside of being car-dependent, of course, is having to frequently fuel up. When your tank is low, you should hope it happens near this BP station on 17th Avenue in Coconut Grove.

If you've ever taken Spanish lessons, it's safe to say you learned what *carajo* meant outside the classroom. But according to El-Carajo's proprietors, who cite the Royal Academy of Spanish, the term originally referred to the crow's nest atop the mast of an old Spanish caravel. The expletive evolved from being sent to the *carajo* as punishment.

A three-generation family business, El Carajo started as a humble gas station and quickie mart but has expanded over the last 30 years owing to the passions of its owners. Beyond the racks of window cleaner, cigarettes, Altoids, and other convenience-store staples is an unexpected and hidden destination for food and wine lovers. There's an excellent Cuban coffee and pastry bar, stocked with whole cakes and pies, croquettes, and sandwiches, and a brick-encased wine cave outfitted with polished wood counters and a sophisticated international bottle collection that rivals any in Miami. But the real surprise is yet to come.

Pass through the wine room and you'll find yourself in the mural-bedecked dining room of a gourmet restaurant serving traditional Spanish tapas. The menu is extensive and the food is a knockout. Pair your wine selection with the acorn-fed ham, cured for three years, or a classic meat board with serrano ham, manchego cheese, and chorizo; or bring a group of friends and go for the family-style seafood paella.

You'll never judge a gas station by its exterior again.

Address 2465 SW 17th Avenue, Miami, FL 33145, +1 305.856.2424, www.el-carajo.com |
Hours Wine store: 24 hours; restaurant: Mon–Thu noon–10pm, Fri–Sat noon–11pm,
Sun 1pm–9pm; bakery café: Sun–Fri 7am–10pm | Tip If you don't have enough gas to
get to Coconut Grove, fret not! Fill up at another one of Miami's lux gas stations, Europa
Car Wash & Cafe (6075 Biscayne Blvd), serving up free WiFi and a wide array of gourmet
sandwiches in what looks like a hotel lobby on South Beach.

32 El Palacio de los Jugos

Cold drink hot spot

Calle Ocho's reputation as a genuine snapshot of Latin-American life precedes itself. But if you're looking for an unguarded perspective of Latin culture in Miami, head west to Flagami. Calle Ocho turns into 8th Street, the ficus canopies become thinner, and the buildings more neglected. The *Guyabera* and cigar stores are gone, replaced by locksmiths and pawnshops.

Flagami may not have Little Havana's history or charm, but it does have the best, most authentic juice palace in South Florida. Reinaldo and Apolonia Bermudez came to Miami from Cuba in 1965. Reinaldo worked at a grocery store and Apolonia in a factory, all the while saving money over the next five years to open their first Palacio. The establishment started out as a small fruit store in Little Havana and grew into a local empire, currently operating at eight locations in Dade County. The majority of their employees are formerly impoverished Cuban refugees.

There is never a lull in the action at El Palacio. Even at 3 o'clock on a Monday, the place is packed. Outside, under the awning, a man stands behind a kiosk wielding a machete. Fresh, green coconuts on a giant tray are hacked one by one, flipped over onto a funnel, and drained into a jug, ready for sale. Inside, there are hot trays filled with traditional Cuban fare like *arroz con pollo* (chicken and rice) and *platanos* (fried plantains). But the hallmark of the establishment is its busy juice counter, manned by workers clad in bright yellow outfits that match the color of the bananas, passion fruits, and pineapples they squeeze into white Styrofoam cups. You can play it safe and order a delicious fresh-squeezed *limonada* or *jugo de naranja*, but go ahead and be adventurous. For something sweet, try a mamey juice, which tastes a lot like liquid pecan pie. Or cool down with a refreshing guava juice; still sweet, but it won't leave you thirstier than before you drank it.

Address 5721 W Flagler Street, Miami, FL 33144, +1 305.262.0070, www.elpalaciodelosjugos.com | Hours Mon–Sat 8am–9pm, Sun 8am–8pm | Tip Before getting a juice at El Palacio, stop in for a meal at the 94th Aero Squadron restaurant (1395 NW 57th Ave). Watch planes take off and land at one of the world's busiest airports while you dine.

33 Ernest Hemingway's Cats

For whom the cat meows

Cordoned off from Whitehead Street by a low-rising brick wall, Ernest Hemingway's home stands exactly as it did when the world-renowned novelist lived in it, from 1931 to 1939. In the dead of summer, the fans whir on the lanai, pushing the humid air around from the rafters above the green lacquered wood floors. Lush palms and shrubs encircle the 19th-century house, where a handful of American literary gems were penned. Harry Morgan captained boats full of contraband between Key West and Havana in *To Have and Have Not* under this very roof. While Hemmingway toiled away at his masterpieces, his six-toed cats kept him company.

In the early years of Hemingway's time in Key West, he met a ship's captain who was passing through the island. The captain had a six-toed cat named Snow White that tickled Hemingway's fancy, so the generous mariner presented "Papa" with the pet. Today, nearly 85 years later, strolling through the gardens are upwards of 50 polydactyl descendants of Snow White. Some nap outside beneath the shade trees, oblivious to the presence of the visitors ogling the writing desk of their ancestors' owner. Others are seen walking along the edge of Hemingway's in-ground pool, the first of its kind in Key West. It's said to have cost an unheard of $20,000 to construct in 1937, the equivalent of over $300,000 in 2015's economy. Hemingway was well aware of the exorbitant nature of the project. At the north side of the pool, he stuck a coin in the wet cement between two flagstones, exclaiming, "Here, take the last penny I've got!"

It's easy to see why Hemingway chose Key West as one of his residences. His wry sense of humor, eccentric personality, and affinity for a stiff drink fit like a glove in the community of hardscrabble fisherman and other literary lights. When asked once why he had so many felines, the writer replied dryly, "One cat just leads to another."

Address 907 Whitehead Street, Key West, FL 33040, +1 305.294.1136, www.hemingwayhome.com | Hours Daily 9am–5pm | Tip Key West is loaded with famous residences. Visit former president Harry Truman's "Little White House" (111 Front St), where Give 'Em Hell Harry wintered while he was in office.

34 Española Way

Pedestrian paradise

In the geographic center of South Beach, in the middle of an Art Deco panorama, sits a Mediterranean esplanade straight out of Nice. Cars here are restricted, so aside from the beaches and narrow sidewalks jammed with humanity, Española Way is the best place in the city to stroll aimlessly, eat, shop, and absorb the scenery.

For more than 80 years, Española Way has unapologetically held its ground even as Miami Beach has become increasingly crowded and demanding of space. Originally intended for Miami Beach's high society, it was designed as a place for the rich and powerful to indulge in the cool ocean breezes of South Beach. The European-inspired seaside architecture that fills this pedestrian playground is coated in pastel shades of pink and accented with green-and-white-striped window awnings. At its entrance from Washington Avenue, the Clay Hotel is famous for once hosting notorious mobster Al Capone.

However beautiful Española Way was, it was not immune to the slow decline of South Beach from the 1950s through the 1980s. The once sparkling artistic representation of a Mediterranean promenade became just another picture of neglect that afflicted the area. People no longer meandered the pathway; paint peeled from the restaurants and hotels that once boomed with business.

Since its revitalization in the 1980s, Española Way has made significant cultural strides that have moved it beyond its days as an exclusive destination for the elite. The street is now alive with cafes, galleries, and even a few yoga studios, all canopied by ficuses and string lights like New York's Little Italy. The Clay Hotel is now partly a hostel, welcoming world travelers and local youths. Movie sets, street performers, photo shoots, and trinket vendors populate the street. Española Way's beauty has been restored to its original splendor – now for the enjoyment of the masses, not just the classes.

35_Fireman Derek's Key Lime Pie

Set your taste buds ablaze

Key lime pie: it's the most popular harmonization of tart and sweet in the food world. Its origins, however, are up for debate. Some say Key lime pie was the late-19th-century creation of "Aunt Sally," the cook of Florida's first millionaire, Bahamian-born William Curry (aka "Rich Bill"). Others say the heralded pie made its first appearance aboard the ships of sponge fisherman, whose slim rations included Key limes, sweetened condensed milk, and eggs. Both parties deserve medals of some sort.

The best Key lime pies are bare bones and executed to perfection; a moist graham-cracker crust, saturated with Key lime juice and topped with South Florida's famous Key lime custard – pale yellow in color, firm but gooey in texture, and cool in temperature. It's a deceptively rich yet refreshing dessert that will demolish any sweet tooth, and fireman Derek Kaplan does it better than anyone else.

Kaplan taught himself how to bake at the age of 15 when he moved in with his father, who had no culinary background. He soon discovered he had a natural talent in the kitchen. Today, while on duty at Miami Firehouse 1 in Downtown, Kaplan is the designated cook for his crew. When he's not busy protecting the people of Miami, he's baking pies at his Wynwood shop, which opened in July 2014. The small cafe's display case is full of temptations, from savory quiches – in flavor combinations such as spinach and feta or barbequed pork with caramelized onions and guava – to desserts like chocolate-dipped flan and rich, creamy cheesecakes. But most patrons come for the signature Key lime pie. Cut through the delicate custard and into the graham-cracker crust beneath. The tang of the Key lime juice perfectly complements the salty sweetness of the crust, exploding on your taste buds in the most simple, magnificent, Floridian way.

Address 2818 N Miami Avenue, Miami, FL 33137, +1 786.703.3623,
www.firemanderekspies.com | Hours Mon–Wed 8am–6pm, Thu–Fri 8am–9pm,
Sat 10am–9pm, Sun 10am–6pm | Tip If you're in the Keys, home of the Key lime, try
a Key lime pie at Blue Heaven (729 Thomas St) in Key West. Topped with a mountain
of meringue, it's a strong contender for the best slice in the Keys.

36_Florida Keys Brewing Company

Ice cold in Islamorada

Citizens of the Keys are among the world's best at the art of taking a load off, and nothing complements a slow, relaxing day on the water better than a frosty pint of beer. On sizzling, steamy afternoons, an air-conditioned room lined with taps sounds more like a necessity than a luxury. Luckily for residents and visitors to the Keys, the craft beer movement that is sweeping the country has made its way to Islamorada.

Opened in 2015, the fledgling Florida Keys Brewing Company is already well on its way to becoming a regional institution. Owners Cheryl and Craig McBay are devoted to providing top-notch craft beer and were given the tools to succeed in South Florida's burgeoning beer scene by local established breweries like Funky Buddha, in Oakland Park; Saltwater Brewery, in Delray Beach; and Miami Brewing Company, based out of Schnebly's Winery in Homestead – crowdsourcing everything from tips on recipes to successfully marketing their product.

Aside from giving the McBays a solid foundation on which to build their business, these Florida breweries, along with a number of well-established national craft beer companies, donated hundreds of bottle caps for an art project now installed in the McBays' taproom. The walls on either side of the entrance are a mosaic of bottle caps, in ornate, swirling designs.

The bar's backdrop comprises the shades of a typical Keys sunset; yellows, oranges, and blues offset the row of taps beckoning to be pulled. When the breeze dies down and the sun is directly overhead, grab a cold, refreshing SunSessional IPA, with a floral, hoppy aroma and bitter, citrus taste. When the oppressive heat gives way to the ocean breeze later in the day, order a sumptuous coffee stout, the Keys' alternative to a *café con leche*. For a liquid dessert, try the Key lime witbier.

Address 200 Morada Way, Islamorada, FL 33036, +1 305.916.5206, www.floridakeysbrewingco.com | Hours Daily noon–10pm | Tip Complement your beer with some modern American gastropub fare at oo-tray (80900 Overseas Hwy), a few blocks south on the ocean side of US 1. Their menu features unique dishes, both small and large, like the Foie French Toast with frozen, grated foie gras, and a Red Bull reduction.

37 __Florida Keys Wild Bird Rehabilitation Center

Wings on the mend

In the heart of Tavernier, on the west side of Overseas Highway, an ornithological oasis sits shrouded among thickets of dense Florida hollies. A wide variety of wild birds seek refuge here; from parrots and pelicans to songbirds and snow owls. Free of an admission charge, Laura Quinn's Wild Bird Sanctuary flaps and chirps its way into visitors' generous hearts and curious minds.

After visitors rumble down a dusty, rocky driveway, Fredricka, the director's pet green Amazon parrot, greets them from her cage with a pleasant "Hello." A winding boardwalk within the mangroves guides birdwatchers through the numerous aviaries scattered about the grounds. Barred and great horned owls are the first species you'll pass. The great horned's piercing yellow eyes are gaunt with distress; the birds at the sanctuary are all either injured or displaced. The proud broad-winged hawks survey their surroundings perched atop tall branches. A red-shouldered hawk is nearby in its cage, boasting a rust-colored breast and striped brown-and-white wings. Turkey vultures lurch and leer with patchy scarlet faces and black feathers, like the menacing skeksis from *The Dark Crystal*. A tiny red eastern screech owl cozies up within its small house, peeking its head out half sleepily, half vigilantly.

A large mesh aviary sits near the west end of the sanctuary, housing huge-billed brown pelicans, orange-faced and eyelashed double-crested cormorants, and sleek-strutting white ibises. The laughing gulls guffaw from the cage next door, cohabitating with their royal tern roommates.

At the end of the sanctuary, a beautiful open beach is the unbridled preserve for the transient bird population. Free to come and go as they please, pelicans and ibises bask in the sun of the Florida Keys, much like the people who live there.

Address 93600 Overseas Highway, Tavernier, FL 33070, +1 305.852.4486, www.keepthemflying.org | Hours Daily sunrise–sunset | Tip South Florida is one of the premier bird-watching locations in the country. Along Overseas Highway, look for brown signs indicating stops on the Great Florida Birding and Wildlife Trail where you can pull over and look out for different indigenous birds.

'To save our birds from hook and line injuries'

38 Fruit & Spice Park

Fruit, spice, and everything nice

Miami boasts a variety of flora unlike anywhere else in the country. Banyan trees, saw palmettos, and coconut palms flourish in the region's tropical climate. In the rural Redlands of southern Dade County, a natural park was created for the sole purpose of showcasing the diversity of fruits grown in South Florida. Sausage-shaped fruit drips from the kigelia trees alongside a spraying fountain. A Mediterranean herb garden is alive with the pungent smell of rosemary. Bees buzz in search of nectar. The Fruit & Spice Park, in Miami's rural Redlands, offers a deliciously aromatic experience.

Start by sampling pieces of exotic fruit available inside the welcome area. Discover how the subtle sweetness of a black raspberry complements the powerful tartness of a Pakistan mulberry. Cleanse your palate with a nutty mamey sapote, then compare it to a similarly flavored eggfruit, aptly named since its texture resembles the yolk of a hard-boiled egg. Wrap up your tasting journey with the mellow citrus notes of a fuzzy yellow loquat and the tang of a star apple, with its bright white flesh and magnificently colored purple rind.

The flowering trees scattered around the park bloom at different times throughout the year and so the menu of available fruits varies seasonally. You won't find mango in winter or sapodilla in summer, for instance.

The park itself is a cross section of exotic fruits and spices from around the world. Wander through the sugar cane and banana grove native to South America. Macadamia nuts grow plump inside large green pods hanging from the macadamia tree, while red clusters of lychees dangle from their branches as they would in southern China.

As delicious as their fruits look and taste, plucking them off the trees is strictly prohibited. However, if you're lucky enough to find something that's fallen to the ground, having it as an on-the-spot snack is perfectly acceptable.

Address 24801 SW 187th Avenue, Homestead, FL 33031, +1 305.247.5727, www.fruitandspicepark.org | Hours Daily 9am–5pm | Tip Has your visit to the park inspired you to plant some fruit trees of your own? Visit Treeworld Wholesale (24605 SW 192 Ave), which offers a staggering selection of trees and shrubs for purchase, from royal poinciana to Tabebuia.

39 Los Gallos of Calle Ocho

Cuban humility

Roosters are held in the same regard in Cuba as bald eagles are in America. Jose Marti, one of the world's most prolific writers and one of Cuba's favorite sons, secured the legacy of the rooster as a symbol of strength in humility within Cuban society. According to Marti, roosters are a subtle reminder not to seek acceptance by following the latest trends. Just as a rooster succeeds by strutting around with his chest puffed out, you must forge ahead and create your own unique path to fulfillment.

The symbol of the rooster rose to prominence in 16th-century Seville, Spain, centuries before Marti became a national hero. In the small municipality of Moron de la Frontera, there lived a local governor who had claimed he was the "only rooster in Moron." According to him, there was nobody cockier. "Where this rooster crows," he said, "no other dares." The people of Moron de la Frontera took revenge on their oppressor and lynched him, cementing the legend of Moron's Rooster: *Keep pushing your luck / you'll be featherless with one cluck / like the rooster of Moron / when finally comes the dawn.* Today, in Moron, Cuba, a large rooster statue sits in the city square, plucked and humbled.

Chickens are commonly seen wandering around the front lawns of homes in Miami's Little Havana. *Los Gallos de la Calle Ocho* – six-foot multicolored rooster statues found perched outside establishments, from a local pub to a day-care center – are enshrined along the sidewalks of Little Havana's main thoroughfare. Although many of *Los Gallos* have been vandalized, the markings only add depth to the allegory. The statues themselves encapsulate both Marti and Moron's interpretations. Their brilliant exteriors display Cuba's pride and bravado, but beneath their illustrious feathers, while bearing the scars of vandals, a vitiated, flightless bird stands alone, humbled yet independent.

Address Scattered along Calle Ocho (SW 8th Street, Miami, FL, 33135), with notable statues in front of El Pub (1548 SW 8th St) and Goodwill (982 SW 8th St) | Tip The Goodwill on Calle Ocho at the intersection of SW 10th Ave and SW 8th St is one of the more impressive Goodwills in the country. The split-level mega-discount store features a huge and always-changing selection of cheap outfits and used knickknacks.

40__ Green Turtle Inn

Sid and Roxie's Islamorada institution

In 1935, the notorious Labor Day Hurricane, the strongest storm to ever make landfall in the United States, swept through the Florida Keys and ravaged everything in its path. With winds reaching a sustained 185 miles per hour, the 20-foot storm surge washed over the entirety of the Upper Keys, forcing a massive rebuild of streets and railroads. The new Overseas Highway was completed in the early 1940s, and a few years later, Sid and Roxie Siderious bought the former OD King's Rustic Inn, a small hotel and cafe right off the east side of US 1 in Islamorada. Their establishment became an instant hit with local fisherman and travelers. Since 1947, Sid and Roxie's Green Turtle Inn has been offering some of the Key's most delicious and hearty fare, serving its famous turtle chowder with a side of pepper sherry.

The Green Turtle harvested more than 6,000 pounds of turtle meat per month, canning thousands of servings of turtle soup in their cannery and serving up their famous fresh turtle steaks, soups, and chowders in-house, until 1993, when the consumption of turtle meat became illegal in the US. Though the "turtle" chowder on the menu no longer contains actual turtle meat, whatever's in it is surely just as delicious.

Beyond the mock reptilian cuisine, the Green Turtle offers classic Keys delicacies done right. Sample the savory scallops and clams plucked from the waters surrounding the restaurant or indulge in a heaping serving of fresh, local conch that is flash-fried and sandwiched on warm bread over a thin layer of mango mayonnaise.

People flock to Florida and the Keys for the beautiful – albeit hot – weather, the laid-back vibes that emanate from the white-sand beaches, and the unparalleled seafood. In Islamorada, the sport fishing capital of the world, this landmark eatery calls mile marker 81.2 its home.

Address 81219 Overseas Highway, Islamorada, FL 33036, +1 305.664.2006, www.greenturtlekeys.com | Hours Tue–Sun, 7am–2pm, 5pm–10pm | Tip In the days of yore, the Green Turtle used to offer "Key West pinks" (shrimp) steamed in beer. Although the pinks aren't on the menu anymore, they still exist in the waters around the Keys. Considered to be the sweetest of all crustaceans, it is well worth your time to go fishing for these critters, or pick some up at one of the area's many seafood markets.

41 Greynolds Park

Miami's Mount Everest

If South Florida had a human face in the early part of the 20th century, it would've been pockmarked by a rash of rock quarries where massive amounts of limestone and coral had been extracted from beneath its skin. But much like a teenage diamond in the rough, the region went on to embrace its scarred past and find beauty in its imperfections. Greynolds Park, for instance, a rock quarry in its younger years, has since been transformed into a bucolic "mountain" of nature.

Florida's hills only reach so far south. From the northernmost parts of the state, its rolling terrain breaks around Orlando, where the gently undulating topography abruptly falls as flat as a pancake. All of South Florida was once part of the Everglades – its wetlands deemed unsuitable for building until the 19th century, when people figured out how to drain the marshes. Once the area's coral and limestone foundation was exploited and railroads made their way south, the region transitioned from uninhabitable marshland to one of the country's biggest metropolitan areas – in less than a century.

Thanks to the old quarry, the highest point in South Florida is Greynolds Park's coral fortress, which sits atop a 42-foot mound created by the massive burial of old mining equipment. Views from the fortress, with its American flag fluttering in the breeze overhead, offer a unique perspective of the level, tri-county area, which can't otherwise be easily glimpsed.

Soak up the sunshine above the old-growth trees that shade the park. Watch the children walk their bicycles up to the fortress and race them down, shrieking with excitement. Explore the park's bird rookery, mangrove boardwalk, covered bridge, and lagoon. Sitting here amid the picnic tables, grass fields, and Southern oaks in the damp heat of North Miami, you might almost imagine yourself in old Dixie instead.

Address 17530 West Dixie Highway, North Miami Beach, FL 33160, +1 305.945.3425, www.miamidade.gov/parks/greynolds | Hours Daily sunrise–sunset | Tip There is no shortage of golf courses in South Florida. Rent some clubs and play a quick 9 at "twilight" (2pm during standard time and 3pm during daylight savings) for less than $20 at Greynolds Park's public course.

42 — Hanging Gardens at Perez Art Museum

Babylon by the bay

Nestled on the southwest corner of the MacArthur Causeway, overlooking Biscayne Bay, is one of the city's preeminent modern architectural feats, appropriately bearing the name of Miami condo-magnate Jorge Perez. A giant wooden pergola, with beams running parallel to the shoreline below, hangs over architects Herzog and de Meuron's steel, concrete, and glass masterpiece. Opened in 2013, the Perez Art Museum, just like the installations inside, is a work of art.

Even the parking lot is something to be admired. The gravel below and concrete above blend seamlessly with the entrance to the building, which leads you up a flight of stairs and through a simulated rain forest, with water slowly trickling down each side of the staircase. From the mezzanine, it's impossible to miss the massive, 20-foot vertical gardens harnessed to the beams above. Tremendous botanical columns bursting with more than 200 species of ferns and flowering plants gently sway with the sea breeze. Cacti and flowering salvia add texture and color, attracting birds and bees to the greenery.

The columnar gardens are the brainchild of the brilliant French botanist Patrick Blanc, who designed Madrid's famed vertical garden. Herzog and de Meuron were stunned by Blanc's mastery, and were dead set on bringing him to Miami to fill PAMM's exterior with life. Plants that flourish in the dark grow under the shade of the pergola, facing the museum, while sturdier florae that are better able to withstand the elements face the bay. Within the hanging gardens, on the back patio, swinging seats with steel-mesh backrests overlook Biscayne Bay and Miami's port. Somewhere between a rocking chair and a hammock, the most comfortable work of art ever invented begs guests to take a seat, relax in the shade, and breathe in the salt air.

Address 1103 Biscayne Boulevard, Miami, FL 33130, +1 305.375.3000, www.pamm.org | Hours Thu 10am–9pm, Fri–Tue 10am-6pm | Tip The Bass Museum (2100 Collins Ave) in Miami Beach also specializes in contemporary art. The building was once the city's public library and is a prime example of the area's Art Deco architecture.

43___Haulover Cut
The gateway to Miami's watershed

The turquoise waters and white sands along the inlet at Haulover set an idyllic scene for beachgoers. Fishing boats and private motorboats churn their way in and out of this narrow stretch of water, which connects the ritzy northern stretch of Biscayne Bay to the Atlantic Ocean. But what makes this spot special is neither the beautiful setting nor the commuting boats, but its crucial role in the history of Miami's drug trade. Haulover Cut was once the gateway for the influx of drugs that permanently changed Miami's urban landscape.

In the 1970s and 1980s, when the demand for marijuana and especially cocaine skyrocketed in the States, Miami was targeted as the primary entry point for narcotics arriving from South and Central America. The cartels pumped exorbitant amounts of illegal substances into the city by boat, and with the drugs came the exchange of billions of dollars. Soon, Miami became a mecca for people who had affinities for both.

The success of the cartels' operation hinged upon the infrastructure surrounding this single inlet. Upper floors of posh apartment buildings built during the heyday of the cocaine rush provided prime lookout posts to determine when illicit cargo could be brought ashore without attracting attention. Miami officials – both police and Coast Guard – were notoriously corrupt at the time, allowing drug runners relative freedom to carry on their business.

Haulover Cut was the main vein to Miami's racing, drug-addled heart. The ramifications from the illegal activity were smeared daily across the front page of the *Miami Herald*. Mall shootings and diners being taken hostage at posh restaurants were regular occurrences during the "Scarface years." From those atrocities, however, rose Miami's vibrant, sophisticated, and diverse cityscape. For better or for worse, it's "the city that cocaine built."

Address Haulover Park, 10800 Collins Avenue, Miami Beach, FL 33154, +1 305.947.3525, www.miamidade.gov/parks/haulover | Hours Daily sunrise to sunset | Tip Arrive by boat or rent one and go for a tour or fishing with a guide at Captain Jay's (10800 Collins Ave) at the south end of the park.

44 Hialeah Park

The sport of kings for those who aren't

Vanderbilts and Whitneys came here to place their bets. World leaders Winston Churchill and John F. Kennedy strolled the concourses. For almost a century, Hialeah Park has held court in Central Dade County. Though the racetrack, just like the neighborhood, has become a bit scuffed around the edges, it remains an exquisite gem that still draws the kings of Miami.

Scenes from the films *The Godfather Part II* and *The Champ* were shot here because of the park's unheralded beauty. Curving coral staircases awash in vines wind up to the grandstand, with white-wooded breezeways that have remained untouched through the years. Designated an Audubon Bird Sanctuary, the park hosts a flock of flamingos that can be seen loitering around the infield lake or flying en masse to the other side later in the day to catch the last of the sun's rays. The well-groomed walking ring, lined with neatly trimmed hedges, snakes from the paddock through the main entrance; human traffic halts to watch the quarter horses trot by only to disappear into the depths of the stable underneath the shimmering white rafters.

The bugle player trumpets "First Call," indicating it's time to post. The horses, mounted by jockeys wearing bright silks that glisten in the South Florida sunshine, are paraded in front of onlookers of all ages. As the horses are positioned in the starting gate, anticipation builds exponentially among the loyal fans who routinely flock to Hialeah Park. With the blast of a gun and an alarm bell, they're off. Elderly Hispanic men scream obscenities at the horses and their jockeys, slamming their rolled-up race programs in frustration and anticipation. In a span of fifteen seconds from start to finish, the thundering hooves rush by. At the end of the race, gamblers run as fast as the horses they've just bet on to the teller windows to collect their winnings – or attempt to recoup their losses by betting the next race.

Address 2200 E 4th Avenue, Hialeah, FL 33013, +1 305.885.8000, www.hialeahparkcasino.com. | Hours Sun–Thu 9am–3am, Fri–Sat open 24 hours | Tip Races are only held at the park from late December through early March. However, the casino is open year round.

45 History of Diving Museum

20,000 leagues into the Keys

Just a few blocks from both the Atlantic Ocean and the Gulf of Mexico, the History of Diving Museum showcases an overwhelming assortment of nautical equipment that spans hundreds of years of technological evolution. The museum was founded in 2005 by two marine biologists, husband and wife Joe and Sally Bauer, to give their extraordinary collection a permanent home. Enter the exhibit through the faux airlock in the museum's lobby, and step into a dank maze of diving apparatuses. Stage lights spotlight every object on display, from cages to breathing tubes. Life-sized mannequins adorned in diving attire from centuries ago dangle from the ceiling behind Plexiglas walls. Take a seat inside Dr. Halley's diving bell, an upside-down bell-shaped tank used to transport undersea explorers, and release the air valves. Experience how much pressure an early-20th-century diver would have felt attempting to completely submerge an old diving helmet; it's harder than it looks.

The crown jewel of the museum is, undoubtedly, the hall of diving helmets. Nearly 50 rare diving masks from all over the world, from Greece to Japan, are presented behind a glass case. Copper masks with grate- and glass-covered viewfinders are arranged in a grid, completely covering the wall in front of you. Press the button on the podium in front, and watch each mask light up in sync with its audio presentation.

The History of Diving Museum is an experience unique to the Florida Keys. Cities like Paris and London are steeped in the culture of an intellectual society, as museums like the Louvre and Tate Modern attest. In the Keys, life sighs and forgets about couth. Instead of gazing at an abstract piece of contemporary art for hours and analyzing it for commentary on the social condition, residents of the Keys look at the gobs of diving stuff and say aloud, "Well, would you look at that!"

Address 82990 Overseas Highway, Islamorada, FL 33036, +1 305.664.9737, www.divingmuseum.org | Hours Daily 10am–5pm | Tip Speaking of diving, up the road in Key Largo you'll find Jules' Undersea Lodge (51 Shoreland Dr), a hotel 21 feet beneath the lagoon's surface. Guests must be scuba certified (classes offered at the lodge).

46 HM69 Nike Missile Base

On the brink of world destruction

In the bowels of the Everglades, 20 miles southwest of the middle of nowhere, three ominous silos stand dormant in fields of waving cattails and saw grass. These silos, the only Nike Hercules Missile site still remaining in South Florida, once housed nuclear warheads and missiles that fired faster than a speeding bullet. One false move from either president or premier could have spelled the end for the United States, Russia, and probably the world.

In response to a botched Bay of Pigs Invasion and with American missiles stationed within range of Moscow, the Soviet Union had decided to transport missiles to its communist ally in the Caribbean – Cuba, where Fidel Castro had been in power for less than five years. In October 1962, the entire planet was just 15 minutes away from Armageddon. At the height of the Cold War, the Soviets dug in their heels in a nuclear standoff against America a mere 90 miles away from US shores. For two weeks, while the globe held its collective breath, South Florida was the warm, beachy frontline for a pending nuclear disaster.

The Nike missile silos were built two years after the Cuban Missile Crisis, making the Everglades the United States' first line of defense from the country's closest communist enemy. The base was functional for 15 years, with more than 10 missiles always aimed south toward Havana, ready to intercept and destroy any incoming object in minutes. Since 1979, the site has been operated by Everglades National Park. Sitting on an unkempt road, surrounded by a barbed wire fence with a padlocked gate, the HM69 Nike Missile Base can only be toured with a park ranger. More than fifty years after its construction, behind a set of giant aluminum sliding doors, in a rusty barn overgrown with weeds, a single restored missile is all that's left; an explosive steel reminder of how fragile tranquility can be.

Address 40001 State Highway 9336, Homestead, FL 33034, +1 305.242.7700, www.nps.gov/ever/learn/historyculture/hm69.htm | Hours Dec–Apr; times vary, call ahead to schedule a guided tour | Tip While you're in the park, head to the Anhinga Trail. Great for walking and biking, this trail offers unique views of areas deep in the Everglades, mostly untouched by humans.

47 __ Holocaust Memorial
Hand of God

In comparison to the rest of the country, Miami, specifically Miami Beach, has a considerable Jewish population. In the neighborhood south of 5th Street (now known as the Art Deco District) where Jews were permitted to live after World War II, it wasn't uncommon to find survivors with concentration camp numbers tattooed on their arms. "Gentiles Only" signs were once posted on many properties throughout Miami Beach. Though painful to imagine, the former Gulf Hotel actually carried the slogan, "Always a view, never a Jew." Over the years, the Jewish population steadily increased as anti-Semitic laws were repealed. In the 1980s, Miami Beach's population was 62 percent Jewish, with over 60,000 residents in Jewish households. Although the proportion isn't as high today, the area is still home to an active Jewish community.

On city blocks 1933 through 1945 (the exact years of the Nazis' reign in Germany) along Meridian Avenue, a memorial designed by artist Kenneth Treister stands four stories tall and symbolizes "a suffering that transcends suffering," as Elie Wiesel, Holocaust survivor and author of *Night*, called it. A monumental arm with a tattooed Auschwitz identification number breaks through the ground and reaches toward the sky. Clinging for life to the powerful limb are dozens of naked men, women, and children in visible agony and despair. Fifty granite slabs surround the sculpture, inscribed with the names of thousands of Jews who were murdered during World War II. A circular reflecting pool sets the tone for contemplation and remembrance.

The memorial stands in stark contrast to the warm, breezy temperament of Miami Beach, which makes its impact all the greater. It serves as a chilling and emotional reminder of the atrocities that occurred and offers a sanctuary for reflection. An inscription on the wall reads simply: *Meet the horrible truth and be shattered. – Anne Frank*

Address 1933–1945 Meridian Avenue, Miami Beach, FL 33139, +1 305.538.1663, www.holocaustmemorialmiamibeach.org | **Hours** Daily 9:30am–sunset | **Tip** Visit the nearby Jewish Museum (301 Washington Ave). The building was the first synagogue on Miami Beach.

48 I-95 Express Lanes

You get what you pay for

Heat and humidity aren't the only things locals seek relief from. Traffic in Miami rivals the worst of Los Angeles and New York City. I-95, Dade County's clogged artery, attempts to carry the motorized blood flow in and out of the city. Unfortunately, the traffic gods have frowned upon this stretch of highway for decades. Warnings from Google Maps almost always arrive too late to pull you out of the mess you'll find yourself in any time before 11pm.

After years of increasing congestion and frustration, the interstate was finally shunted in 2010 by the Florida Department of Transportation. The two far left lanes in both directions were sectioned off by a line of equally spaced plastic barriers, intended to keep traffic flowing for long stretches in northern Dade County, where traffic is otherwise unbearable. Starting from the Golden Glades interchange and extending all the way to Downtown, traffic idles and halts for what feels like forever in the regular lanes, but in the express lanes, feel the schadenfreude flow freely as you whiz by the bumper-to-bumper masses. Getting to ride in what seems almost like your own private lane does come with a VIP cost, though. When traffic is at its worst, expect to shell out upwards of $6. You can't necessarily put a price tag on sanity, but if you could, you'd better believe it would be more than the toll.

Driving in Miami has its own unique qualities. Being cut off is like someone waving hello. So if you're tucked into an express lane, don't believe for a second that those plastic cones will keep traffic in the slow lanes from swerving into yours. The more crowded the highway, the crazier the maneuvers, so take a defensive stance and expect the unexpected.

At your next stop for gas, go ahead and pick up a SunPass, the transponder used to electronically pay the express lane tolls. You'll need it even if you just want to make a quick escape to Georgia.

Address The I-95 Express Lanes run from the Golden Glades interchange to Downtown Miami. | Tip You can buy a SunPass at any gas station around town. Keep in mind, however, that the express lanes run straight through from the Golden Glades to Downtown without any exits in between, so if your destination is on that stretch, you'll have to either loop back around after you get off the express route or skip the express lanes altogether and tough out the traffic.

49___Ichimura Japanese Garden

Secret sanctuary on Watson Island

Watson Island is the concrete slab that sits in the middle of Biscayne Bay, just across from the mainland off the MacArthur Causeway. Though home to Jungle Island and the Miami Children's Museum as well as an old seaplane base, an outboard club, and a public boat ramp, for the most part, the island is just a checkpoint on the way to Miami Beach. But tucked away in between the causeway and Jungle Island's parking garage, without any noticeable signage, is a beautiful Japanese garden cloaked by orchid trees and bamboo stalks.

Planted in 1961, the gardens are among Watson Island's oldest residents. The idea was hatched by Japan native Kiyoshi Ichimura, founder of Ricoh Company, who visited Miami in 1957 for a camera exhibition. From his hotel window, he noted the contrast between the lush vegetation of Miami and the barrenness of the island's terrain. Ichimura remarked to a city commissioner how beautifully hundreds of cherry trees would transform Watson Island. The wheels were put in motion to bring the flowering trees to Miami, but unfortunately they could not be transported due to potentially harmful bacteria. Instead, hundreds of orchid trees were imported from China by Ichimura as a gift, and were soon planted. The concept of placing a traditional Japanese garden among them began to take form when Ichimura sent a team of carpenters and gardeners from the Land of the Rising Sun to the Magic City.

Despite a slight relocation upon the installation of Jungle Island, the garden's beautiful tranquility remains the same as it ever was. A cascading waterfall stifles the sound of traffic passing over the causeway. Lily pads rest in their elevated pond while water trickles from one level down into the next. A neatly combed rock garden offers an environment for introspection and meditation. Keep your eyes peeled when hunting for this small sanctuary. It's easy to miss, but hard to forget.

Address 1101 MacArthur Causeway, Watson Island, FL 33139, +1 305.960.4639, www.friendsofjapanesegarden.com | **Hours** Daily 9am–6pm | **Tip** For more Japanese-Miami fusion, head to Pubbelly on Miami Beach (1418 20th St). Pubbelly offers inventive Japanese tapas like short-rib-and-corn dumplings.

50 InterContinental's Dancer

Hold me closer light-up dancer

In a city full of world-class unique architecture, the extraordinarily plain InterContinental Hotel is something of wallflower. By day, the building is a bland beige monolith looming over the shores of Biscayne Bay. It's dwarfed by the jagged-roofed Southeast Financial Center and nowhere near as beautiful as the chrome multileveled Miami Tower. But when the sun sets and Downtown lights up with every color on the spectrum, the InterContinental does more than just steal the show, it creates its own.

What the InterContinental lacks in aesthetic individuality during the day, it makes up for in sex appeal at night. A silhouette of a buxom woman, 19 stories tall, dances provocatively on the front of the hotel, flipping her hair seductively, drawing stares from anyone in eyeshot. Her background changes from red to yellow to green to blue. All the while, she bends over, bounces up and down, and twirls around, without leaving much to the imagination. She's the stripper of Miami's skyline.

The either-love-her-or-hate-her silhouetted dancing girl came onto the scene in 2012 via a $30 million renovation to the InterContinental; at the very least, the effort put into the project is what makes this bawdy spectacle something to behold. More than 90,000 pixels and 300,000 LEDs comprise the "digital canvas." It was christened by none other than *Entourage's* Jeremy Piven, whose character Ari Gold is, in many ways, a personification of Miami itself: superficial at first glance, but upon further investigation, found to possess an undervalued depth.

Every year, the hotel hosts a competition to select a new dancer to grace their LED facade based on both talent and their passion and dedication to their city. Though men are officially eligible to audition, the winners so far have all been rather svelte women. Maybe it's just a coincidence.

Address 100 Chopin Plaza, Miami, FL 33131, +1 305.577.1000, www.icmiamihotel.com |
Hours Daily sunset–sunrise | Tip Taking a walk around Bayfront Park, adjacent to the
InterContinental, is a great way to pass the time while waiting for the sun to set. This is the
main hub for the Ultra Music Festival, one of the world's largest EDM and house music
events in the world, held in late March.

51 Jackie Gleason's Mausoleum

Ralph Kramden's last stop

Miami is brash, unabashed, and adored by many, much like one of its most famous former residents, Jackie Gleason. Gleason, dubbed the "Great One" by film legend Orson Welles, spent most of the latter half of his life here. For much of the 1960s, he was the city's unofficial mayor, broadcasting the *Jackie Gleason Show* "from Miami Beach, the sun and fun capital of the world."

The inspiration for the cartoon caveman Fred Flintstone, Gleason's Ralph Kramden in *The Honeymooners* was an unapologetically blunt and boastful character who took the nation by storm in 1955. His endearing showmanship and impressive spontaneity on and off the set carried him to superstardom in less than a year, the entire duration of the show. Gleason was a behemoth among men in the newly formed sphere of television entertainment, and CBS concocted different ways to keep him on the air.

In 1964, after 14 years on the tube, Gleason's own variety program, the eponymous *Jackie Gleason Show*, moved to Miami Beach at his request. Gleason was clearly in the driver's seat (his show's ratings were demolishing the competition), and when he insisted on filming closer to his home, CBS had no choice but to acquiesce. Miami Beach was soon thrust into the limelight; its shoreline was showcased in the series' opening scene, and Gleason ended many episodes declaring, "As always, the Miami Beach audience is the greatest audience in the world!"

To this day, Gleason's legacy is seen in Miami and its beaches. His variety hour was broadcast from the former Miami Beach Auditorium, now the Fillmore Miami Beach at Jackie Gleason Theater, Miami's premier event venue. Today, his white marble mausoleum stands alone at Our Lady of Mercy Catholic Cemetery. The words of his most famous catchphrase are inscribed at its base: "And away we go."

"AND AWAY WE GO"

Address 11411 NW 25th Street, Miami, FL 33172, +1 305.592.0521 | Hours Daily 7am–5:30pm | Tip One thing Miamians do well is shop. Doral, the neighborhood where the cemetery is located, is very suburban and residential. However, there are two significant shopping venues: the Dolphin Mall and Miami International Mall. The more popular Dolphin Mall (11401 NW 12th St), is a tremendous outlet shopping center encompassing more than 1 million square feet.

52_ The Jewel Box
Elevator to heaven

For 42 years, Bacardi's American corporate offices were located in Midtown Miami on Biscayne Boulevard. Although the famous spirits company has since relocated to Coral Gables, its landmarked former headquarters is now home to the National YoungArts Foundation, and remains the crown jewel of the Modern Architecture district.

The floral- and tropical-themed *azulejos* (blue and white tin-glazed ceramic tilework) that run up the sides of the seven-story Bacardi tower feature abstract representations of birds and plants native to the area. Commissioned by Bacardi's then-president José "Pepin" Bosch and designed by exiled Cuban architect Enrique Gutierrez in 1964, Bacardi USA was established five years after Fidel Castro assumed power in Cuba.

Behind the taller main building sits a smaller rectangular structure, three stories high and cantilevered above a huge Bacardi bat logo enameled onto the courtyard tiles. Bacardi commissioned this floating cube, wrapped in colorful stained glass "tapestries," in 1972. The work, completed by German artist Johannes Dietz, depicts the rum-making process, from raw sugarcane to the finished product. Inside the building, however, the design takes on a completely different life.

At the base of the Bacardi Annex, underneath the shade of the overhang, sits an unassuming elevator that lifts you to the second and third floors. The doors open to reveal a rainbow of light, welcoming you inside Miami's life-sized jewelry box. The sun brilliantly illuminates the crystalline walls, and seen from this perspective, the glass mosaic looks like a wildly colored island paradise. Yellows, oranges, and ruby reds bounce off the ceilings and floors, gleefully dancing with emerald greens and sapphire blues, as if the fiery silhouette of a setting sun is tangling with the deep azure of the ocean beneath. And standing in the middle of it all, you are the gem inside.

Address 2100 Biscayne Boulevard, Miami, FL 33137 | **Tip** La Provence (2200 Biscayne Blvd), one of Miami's best French cafes, is just a block north on Biscayne. After basking in the rainbow inside the Bacardi Annex, grab a croissant and continue exploring the rest of Midtown Miami.

53 John Pennekamp Coral Reef State Park

Underwater playground

The only living coral barrier reef in North America teems with marine life at Pennekamp Park, just three miles off the shores of Key Largo. A sanctuary for fish, sea mammals, and polyps alike, the waters at Pennekamp are protected, housing the Great Florida Reef, the third largest coral barrier reef system in the world. The spectacular snorkeling destination attracts everyone from young children to senior citizens, who take a short boat ride to reach the veritable underwater zoo. For marine biologists and those fascinated by sea life, it's a dream come true.

Established in 1963, Pennekamp was the country's first underwater park. John D. Pennekamp, the park's namesake, was an editor for the *Miami Herald* who rose to prominence in the 1940s as the leader of the reactivated Everglades National Park Commission. As much effort as Pennekamp put into establishing Everglades National Park, he put as much, if not more, into establishing Florida's Coral Reef Preserve in response to the unbridled removal of queen conch and coral from the depths of the surrounding waters. In 1960, the wish of Pennekamp and other conservationists was granted when Florida Governor Leroy Collins spearheaded the movement to give control of this 75-square-mile plot of ocean floor to the preserve.

The density of fauna that populates this concentrated undersea parcel of land is staggering. More than 6,000 individual reefs populate the system that runs through Pennekamp Park and beyond. More than 1,000 species of plants and animals call the reef system their home. One of the most surprising subaquatic sites is manmade: Florida's Christ of the Abyss, a bronze statue of Jesus beneath 25 feet of water near the reef, is perpetually traversed by fish ranging from large, shimmering barracudas to tiny yellow-and-black-spotted butterfly fish.

Address 102601 Overseas Highway, Key Largo, FL 33037, +1 305.451.1202, www.pennekamppark.com | Hours Daily 8am–5pm | Tip If you have a desire to snorkel closer to the city, you can easily do so in Biscayne Bay. Smaller coral reefs that also offer spectacular underwater views exist outside of Pennekamp Park, just 10 miles offshore of Miami.

54 __Key West Cemetery
Laugh to death

Amid the craziness that is Key West, one of the country's most ironic cemeteries sits quietly in the middle of Old Town, surrounded by bars, T-shirt shops, and historic residences. On an island practically drowning in piña coladas and rum runners, one would assume a cemetery is the last place anybody would want to visit; nothing shall get in the way of ruining a beachside bender. But much like the island itself, this graveyard has more panache than most others in the country.

Inside the wrought-iron gates, graves and mausoleums are crammed underneath voluminous red poinciana trees. On account of Key West having a high water table as well as being such a small landmass, underground burial in this tiny cemetery is at a premium. Above-ground vaults are predominant. However unique the raised graves are, who's buried in them is even more compelling.

The deceased range from Confederate soldiers to 19th-century Cuban Revolutionaries; from Ernest Hemingway's fishing guide to "General" Abe Sawyer, a carnival midget who requested to be buried in a full-sized casket. B. P. Roberts, a local hypochondriac, is buried with the epitaph, "I told you I was sick." Another nearby gravestone reads, "I'm just resting my eyes." Roosters strut about the grounds, feasting on coconuts recently fallen from their palms, cracked on impact with the headstones beneath. Iguanas munch on weeds sprouting up from crevices in the stone mausoleums, and snack on mosquitos buzzing by.

The spirit of Key West is best heard from street performers that line Duval Street; it's best tasted in a frozen drink from Fat Tuesdays; best seen in the faces of those watching the sunset from Mallory Square; best smelled in the Key lime vapors that flow from Kermit's Key West Lime Shoppe. And it's best felt in the cemetery, where Key West's inherent eccentricity eternally rests.

Address 701 Passover Lane, Key West, FL 33040, +1 305.292.8177, www.friendsofthekeywestcemetery.com | Hours Daily 7am–6pm in winter, 7am–7pm in summer | Tip Key West is known for its oddities and spookiness almost as much as its frozen alcoholic drinks. If you're interested in the supernatural realm, there are a number of "ghost tours" available throughout the city.

55 Knaus Berry Farm

All buns go to heaven

Less than an hour from Downtown, the Redlands is a world apart from Miami and its surrounding urban sprawl. Here, mango trees, tomato patches, and orange groves outnumber humans in one of South Florida's few remaining agricultural areas. Where Miami has white-sand beaches and shimmering condo buildings, the Redlands have fresh fruit stands and sugar-cane fields. This far southwest of the city, it's difficult to determine where civilization ends and the Everglades begin.

The Redlands comprise the hot and sweaty "Amish Country" of Dade County. From late fall through the middle of spring, Knaus Berry Farm straddles the line between charming country outpost and gourmet bakery. The plain tin trailer on a blacktop parking lot that marks your arrival is easily overlooked if you're unfamiliar with the area. Friendly Mennonites run the operation. Grab ears of fresh local corn, baskets of strawberries, and tomatoes harvested earlier in the day. Order a cool, refreshing blueberry milkshake from the creamery to combat the scorching South Dade sun. Out back, a U-pick strawberry patch has been filling up with children and their parents for over a half century.

But Knaus Berry Farm's biggest draw isn't its selection of Florida's freshest produce, its timeless strawberry field, or its Mennonite charm. The bakery – specifically the gooey, moist cinnamon buns – is what causes a spike in the Redlands population during the farm's business hours. Patrons sometimes wait for a half hour or longer in a line that snakes around the storefront, through the parking lot, and onto the street. As the aroma of the butter and cinnamon grows stronger, so do your hopes of grabbing a box of sweet, sticky, sugary nirvana. Sink your teeth into the warm, sweet roll that puts even the trendiest bakeries in Manhattan to shame. But don't roll in on a Sunday; the farm is closed for God's day of rest.

Address 15980 SW 248th Street, Homestead, 33031, +1 305.247.0668, www.knausberryfarm.com | Hours Nov–mid-April, Mon–Sat 8am–5:30pm | Tip Also worth a stop is Burr's Berry Farm (12741 SW 216th St), a 10-minute drive northeast. They may not have Knaus's famous cinnamon buns, but their signature strawberry shortcake is nothing to shake a stick at.

56__Lincoln Road Garage
Miami's parking chateau

Finding a parking space on the street in South Beach can sometimes feel like an exercise in madness. Fortunately for Miamians, there's the Lincoln Road Garage, a bold and daring feat of architecture, which offers not only refuge for your car, but places to shop, dine, catch a view of both the city and the ocean, and even live.

Jacques Herzog and Pierre de Meuron, the same team that conceived the Bird's Nest Olympic Stadium in Beijing, the De Young Museum in San Francisco, and Miami's own Perez Art Museum, designed the mixed-use masterpiece that sits on the western end of Lincoln Road Mall. From bottom to top, crooked concrete columns and wedges support the versatile structure, giving it the resemblance of a post-modern house of cards. There are no exterior walls and no two floors are the same. Ramp steepness varies from gentle to sharp, accommodating the range of heights the garage offers per floor. A staircase spirals through the middle of the light-flooded building.

At street level, the garage features eleven shops and restaurants. On the fifth floor, a glass-encased retail space, currently a beauty boutique, is wedged between floating parking lots. On the seventh floor, a tremendous open space with 34-foot-high ceilings and a spectacular wraparound view of South Beach holds events ranging from yoga classes to wine tastings, and can be rented for weddings or private parties. And on the top floor, nestled in what looks like a hole in the roof of the garage, sits a more than 5000-square-foot house; the roots from its hanging garden can be seen dripping into the level below.

The garage's stunning design and utilitarianism come at a steep price. To leave your car in one of the parking palace's 300 spaces will cost you upwards of $20. But like everything else in real estate, the three most important things are: location, location, location.

Address 1111 Lincoln Road, Miami Beach, FL 33139, www.1111lincolnroad.com |
Tip Grab an old-fashioned Southern meal with a modern twist at the up-and-coming
Yardbird Café (1600 Lenox Ave, Miami Beach). The fried chicken with honey hot sauce is
otherworldly.

57 Lock & Load

Say hello to my little friend

Comic Patton Oswalt once described South Florida as "a vestigial sac that America's testosterone and anger drains into." While perhaps that's overstating it a tad, tempers do tend to flare during the long, hot summers of Miami. Hear it on the streets and highways, with horns blaring and expletives flying. See it when someone gets cut in line at a local grocery store. The shade being thrown is a show in itself. Had it not been for the aggression associated with the drug trade in the 1980s, South Florida would not be the booming metropolis it is today.

Those with pent-up frustrations can safely let them all out at Lock & Load – a unique gun range on the fringes of Wynwood's vibrant arts community. Outside, its entrance is bordered by troughs of empty chrome shells like faux mulch in a spice garden. Inside, the lobby's highly polished diamond-plate floors and walls are studded with fully automatic weapons, not to mention a repurposed army helicopter suspended from the ceiling, making the place feel like the vestibule of an FBI arms storage facility.

Before heading into the range, find which guns fit your mood. Visit the front desk to look at the menu of packages. Feeling stealthy? Fire away with the 007 package, featuring firearms like the HK UMP and Glock 18 submachine gun. Patriotic? Go for the Special Forces USA package and pepper your targets with shots from an FN Herstal SCAR. Let your inner Tony Montana loose with the Scarface package and fend off enemy cartels with your IMI Uzi. If themes aren't your deal, go for the aptly named Automatic Gratification, featuring rounds from ten different guns.

Although many prefer to seek mental refuge at the beach or out on the town, for some, Lock & Load provides a much-needed catharsis. After firing your hostilities away, you might just find yourself more tolerant the next time someone cuts you off on I-95.

Address 2545 North Miami Avenue, Miami, FL 33127, +1 305.424.8999,
www.lockandloadmiami.com | Hours Mon–Fri noon–8pm, Sat 11am–8pm,
Sun 11am–6pm | Tip Balance the intensity of target practice with a visit to Art by God
(60 NE 27th St) – an emporium of fossils, minerals, rocks, and other natural treasures.

58 Locust Projects

A young artist's nursery

On the northern fringes of Wynwood, creeping into the Design District, an independent artists' playground exists outside the growing circuit of commercial galleries that runs through Miami. You won't see Ray-Ban tents or Bacardi-sponsored parties at Locust Projects during Art Basel. A-list celebrities don't drop by, either. Instead, you'll find art without frills: an independent outlet for contemporary artists who have "the freedom to experiment with new ideas without the pressures of gallery sales or limitations of conventional exhibition spaces."

Locust Projects got its wings in 1998, more than a decade before real estate mogul Tony Goldman began to develop Wynwood. The idea was hatched in Brooklyn by three Pratt Institute grads who were looking to offer independent artists a venue to showcase site-specific installations. In the late 1990s, Miami's art community was paltry at best, so a warehouse in the city's textile district came relatively cheap. The three artists bought a 3,500-square-foot space between a bus depot and a dilapidated empty lot, across the street from a Salvation Army center in what is now the heart of Wynwood.

Over the years, they have featured a number of Miami-based artists who've used the warehouse as a launching pad, like street artist TYPOE, visual and performance artist Jillian Mayer, and architectural artist Daniel Arsham. Although Locust Projects relocated to the Design District in 2009, it still straddles the line between studio and gallery. The entire interior is redone every month or two to accommodate a new artist's vision. In one show, the artwork may be beneath your feet, with the floors splattered like a Jackson Pollock painting; in the next, industrial fans hang from the ceiling with orange ribbons dangling from each blade. Unlike many galleries that try to keep up with the times, Locust Projects winds its watch to whatever hour it pleases.

Address 3852 N Miami Avenue, Miami, FL 33127, +1 305.576.8570, www.locustprojects.org | Hours Tue–Sat 10am–5pm | Tip Visit another one of Miami's art incubators at Emerson Dorsch (7221 NW 2nd Ave), one of the best exhibition venues in Little Haiti's burgeoning art scene.

59___Lou La Vie

Cruise Miami like a celebrity

If Hertz Rent-a-Car and the Museum of Modern Art had an affair, Lou La Vie would be their love child. Inside this glorious garage, the walls are as decked out as the cars. The space is adorned with hanging pieces of polychromatic pop art, while the showroom floor is covered with automotive masterpieces – from a power-packed Ferrari Scuderia to a Range Rover Sport Autobiography fitted with a satellite radio and state-of-the-art navigational system – any of which can be temporarily yours. As famed travel expert Anthony Bourdain once said about driving around Miami: "This is the one town [where] you won't stick out in a car twenty years too young for you."

Mike Tyson rents from Lou La Vie frequently; a pearl-white Rolls Royce Ghost is one of his personal favorites. Not to be confused with the white Rolls Royce Phantom, one of Jamie Foxx's cars of choice. When Justin Bieber was arrested for drag racing while intoxicated, he was behind the wheel of Lou La Vie's yellow Lamborghini Gallardo. That same Lambo can be yours for a day, a week, whatever you want to spring for.

You may not be a rock star, but rolling up in a multimillion-dollar Bugatti might just make you feel like one. Take a drive down Biscayne Boulevard on a Sunday afternoon. With the bay to the east and civilization to the west, it's a perfect route to see some of the best roadside sights the city has to offer. Cruise through Downtown in the shade of the Icon Brickell and Southeast Financial Center. Head to Bayside and see the beautiful American Airlines Arena, glittering in the afternoon sun. Travel north through the historic district, featuring prominent modern architecture that defined the city in the 1950s and 1960s. Navigating the congested roads of Miami can be as miserable as it is interesting, but even the worst of traffic jams becomes meaningless if you're in the sports car of your dreams.

Address 1444 Biscayne Boulevard, Suite 113, Miami, FL 33132, +1 305.974.1914, www.loulavie.com | Hours Daily 10am–6pm | Tip Roll up to famed chef Michelle Bernstein's restaurant Cena by Michy (6927 Biscayne Blvd). Cena, which means "the most important meal of the day" in Latin, features an "approachable yet adventurous" menu, with dishes like beet sorghum risotto and goat cheese cavatelli.

60 Mack's Fish Camp

The last of the Gladesmen

A hidden gateway to the fruits of the Everglades is tucked away on a small, dusty road in the northwest corner of Dade County. An authentic Gladesmen fishing village on the banks of one of the Everglades' many canals is hard to find, even on the Internet. Driving along the remote Danell Lane, just when you think you are lost, there appear out of nowhere a bait shack, a general store, and a wooden dock under the shade of ficus trees. One of the last remaining family-owned relics of the "urban" Everglades, Mack's Fish Camp is more than the stereotypical airboat stop.

The Jones family has owned and operated Mack's Fish Camp since the late 1930s. Genuine pioneers of the Everglades, the Joneses' first ventured into the Everglades in 1937, when Mack Jones Sr., a farmer, moved westward from what is now North Miami deep into the land of saw grass and alligators. "My great-grandfather was drawn here because of the vast, unexplored land," Marshall Jones says.

Jones squatted the land, farming collards, tomatoes, and other local crops to eventually earn enough money to buy the lot in 1944. He went on to open a general store and bait shack. The legend of Mack's Fish Camp has grown steadily since, serving as both the family's home and a destination for curious visitors seeking a window into the life of a Gladesman.

Children swing on a rope that dangles from a tree branch high above and jump into the murky waters of the channel. "There's no other place I'd rather be," says Marshall. "Just look at my backyard." Sneaky Pete, the family's pet alligator, swims over for a treat: a reward for protecting the children. Airboats roar as they take off from the docks, skipping over small spits of land on their way out to the rich bass fishing grounds. Step into one of the airboats, wave good-bye to Sneaky Pete, and spend a day searching for gators, angling, and getting lost at the Joneses'.

Address Danell Lane, Broward County, FL 33018, +1 888.611.5799, www.macksfishcamp.com | **Hours** Mon–Fri 7am–8pm, Sat–Sun 6:30am–9pm | **Tip** Just up the road, in southwestern Broward County, is Everglades Holiday Park (21940 Griffin Rd, Fort Lauderdale, FL 33332), a less expensive but more touristy version of Mack's Fish Camp. Holiday Park is home base for the television show Gator Boys, and offers airboat tours as well as gator wrestling shows and delicious fried gator tail bites.

61_Mary's Coin Laundry

Wash, fold, drink, repeat

The influence of Cuba in Miami overtakes the senses. The faint smell of cigar smoke permeates the air. Road signs in Spanish are at nearly every intersection. Blaring salsa music through open car windows is the city's soundtrack. On the corner of 27th Avenue and 25th Terrace, on the fringes of Coconut Grove, sits an unassuming laundromat with a Cuban twist. The first clue that this is no ordinary wash-n-fold is the intermingled smell of detergent and coffee that greets you as you approach.

After opening Mary's Coin Laundry in 1982, owner Victor Sanchez, a construction worker and the son-in-law of the eponymous Mary, noticed that young people preferred to wash their clothes late at night. He promptly added a coffee window, and the legend began to take hold.

Now, from morning through evening, washers and dryers rattle and hum alongside espresso machines and blenders. During the daytime, an older clientele populates the laundromat and watches the constant stream of traffic flow by while they wash their clothes. At night and into the wee hours of the morning, Miami's exuberant youth and weary insomniacs pass through to grab some late-night bites and maybe even throw in a load. Police officers, ending their shifts at 5am, stop in for a *pastelito de guayaba* (guava-filled pastry) on their way home.

While it's rare that English is spoken here, you'll find a way to get what you need. The express option is the Cuban coffee staple, the *café con leche* – a shot of sweet, potent Cuban espresso and milk. For those with an appetite, the *medianoche* (Cuban sandwich on egg bread) is a classic. Or to kill that sweet tooth, try a *mamey* (fruit with the taste of an almond-infused pumpkin pie) milk shake. And if you should happen to drip some mustard on your shirt from that *medianoche* you've just devoured, throw it into one of the machines before the stain even has a chance to set.

Address 2542 SW 27th Avenue, Miami, FL 33156, +1 305.443.6672 | **Hours** 24 hours a day | **Tip** For a scenic spot to enjoy your *café con leche*, head south on 27th Ave to its terminus and watch the boats float by from Kenneth Myers Bayside Park.

62 __ Matheson Hammock

A beginner's beach

Swimming is a skill taken for granted by many of South Florida's beachgoers. But if you're not ready for the open ocean or you have kids who are still too young, head to Matheson Hammock's wading beach, where everybody in Miami learns to stay afloat.

Bike or drive through the dark, cool mangrove tunnel that leads to the shallow, doughnut-shaped beach. A man-made atoll pool surrounded by a wispy shoreline has been the unofficial swimming academy of South Miami for more than 80 years. It's the incubator for the city's youngest swimmers – from babies to toddlers; the pond where helpless tadpoles get their legs, lose their tails, and mature into frogs. The education is free. The parking, however, is not.

On weekdays, the essentially empty Matheson Hammock becomes a personal paradise. Launch your boat and head out to sea from the park's marina. Rent a kayak or paddleboard from one of the concession stands. You can even learn how to kiteboard here; harness the sea breeze and shred the calm waters below. Climb the rock formations that cordon off the bowl's calm, shallow waters, which advance into and recede from the pool through submerged vents, directed by the alternating tides. Circumnavigate the waters of this huge saltwater puddle. Set up camp and sprawl out along any stretch of shoreline, moving your towel or chair to align with the sun throughout the day. Palm trees stitch the sand around the edges of the pool, evoking the feel of a desert island. In the distance, downtown Miami's skyline shimmers. Adjust your perspective so that the cityscape lies perfectly between two palms, like a postcard come to life.

Cap off your day of swimming and sunbathing at the elegant Red Fish Grill on the shores of the wading beach. Grab a Corona and a piece of grilled local snapper, and watch the sky fade from pale blue to deep orange to dusk. Class dismissed.

Address 9610 Old Cutler Road, Miami, FL 33156, +1 305.665.5475, www.miamidade.gov/parks/matheson-hammock | Hours Sunrise to sunset (office hours 8am–5pm) | Tip If the Red Fish Grill is too pricey, take Sunset Dr west from Old Cutler and you'll find a variety of unique, more affordable restaurants, like Old Lisbon (5837 Sunset Dr, South Miami) and Shula's 347 Grill (6915 Red Rd, Coral Gables).

63 __ McAlpin Hotel
Quintessential Art Deco

Built in 1940 and designed by Lawrence Murray Dixon, whose other notable works include the Temple House, the Raleigh Hotel, and the Dixon Hotel, the McAlpin is the quintessential example of the Art Deco architecture that has come to define South Beach. Many of the area's hotels were built around this time, all adorned with geometric shapes and sunburst motifs. In the decades that followed, neglect took its toll, eroding nouveau beauties into weathered clunkers. In 1979, Miami Beach's Art Deco District was placed on the National Register of Historic Places, and since then, dozens of buildings like the McAlpin have been completely restored. The people of Miami, and eventually the rest of the world, suddenly took notice of this architectural treasure trove, and South Beach was soon transformed from a quiet community of retirees to a sexy playground for the wealthy and waifish.

Shining with pink, white, and teal – Miami's ubiquitous color scheme – the McAlpin Hotel's tripartite facade featuring three turquoise prongs is the centerpiece of the perfectly symmetrical exterior. Pink concrete awnings, horizontal bars, and large dots accent the trident impeccably against the bright white foundation. The theme continues inside, on the lobby's marbled floors. Beneath jalousie windows and above the front entrance, the deep green McAlpin sign complements the palms and shrubs lining Ocean Drive.

Each morning in South Beach, the sunrise signals the end of yet another raucous night, as partyers stumble their way back from nightclubs like Liv and Story to some of the most famous hotels in the country. At this hour of the morning, the Colony, Carlyle, Cardozo, and Clevelander are full of glitterati pulling down their shades. But at the northern end of Lummus Park, South Beach's most beautiful hotel stands disguised as just another face in a crowd of supermodels.

Address 1430 Ocean Drive, Miami Beach, FL 33139, +1 305.604.8225 | Tip Carnivores rejoice – BLT Steak (1440 Ocean Dr) is a half block north of the McAlpin. Enjoy a fine selection of Wagyu beef inside the grand Betsy Hotel.

64 Mel Fisher Maritime Museum

Today's the day

In 1622, the *Nuestra Senora de Atocha* was headed from Havana back to Spain full of valuable gems and metals from South America; so much precious cargo that it took two months to load and record the inventory. Unfortunately for those on board, a hurricane blew the ship into the reef near the Dry Tortugas, sinking the vessel thirty-five miles west of Key West. More than 350 years later, Mel Fisher discovered the wreck and all the goodies that came with it. Today, you can see the salvage at his Maritime Museum.

Fisher was an Indiana-born hydroelectric engineer turned California-based chicken farmer turned Florida Keys treasure hunter. He made his fortune unearthing underwater valuables and today he is considered to be worth hundreds of millions. A brilliant cross-section of Fisher's career hauls is displayed on two floors of the old Key West Naval Station building, tucked away on the northwest corner of the island. World-class emeralds extracted from the Muzo mines in Colombia and salvaged from the famous *Atocha* wreck glimmer under the lights in the showcase. A small sampling of the 24 tons of silver from the same ship also sparkles on display. Iron shackles from the *Henrietta Marie*, a sunken English merchant-slaver, are exhibited alongside the ship's grand bronze bell – a haunting reminder of the epidemic global slave trade during the 17th and 18th centuries.

For 16 years, Fisher went in nearly daily search – weather permitting – of sunken treasure. Before every venture out to sea, he would exclaim, "Today's the day!" On July 20, 1985, after a relentless search for the *Atocha*, a radio signal to Fisher came in: "Put away the charts. We've got the mother lode!" In an instant, Fisher's childhood dreams – born out of reading Stevenson's *Treasure Island* – came true. His legacy as a modern-day Jim Hawkins lives on.

Address 200 Greene Street, Key West, FL 33040, +1 305.294.2633, www.melfisher.org |
Hours Mon–Fri 8:30am–5pm, Sat–Sun 9:30am–5pm | Tip The Fisher family owns
another museum in Sebastian, on the aptly named Treasure Coast of Florida. Two and
a half hours north of Miami, the Mel Fisher's Sebastian Museum houses yet more items
salvaged from the *Atocha*.

65__Metromover
Miami's monorail

The Miami-Dade County Metromover – free, air-conditioned, comfortable, and offering the best views of many sights in Miami – is an excellent traffic-free way to maneuver through Downtown. Forget having to hunt for an elusive parking spot in the midst of Miami's most densely packed neighborhood, the Metromover chauffeurs you almost anywhere you want to go without having to ride your brakes.

Servicing Downtown since 1986, the Metromover is more like the Monorail at Disney World than a major city's mode of public transportation. Just like its Orlando-based counterpart, it's a great way to traverse parts of the city at your leisure. Temperature controlled electric railcars glide along from Brickell, through Downtown, and into the Omni neighborhood north of the Miami River. The views from the cars are spectacular, riding above traffic and through stations nestled inside buildings. Heading northbound from Museum Park, MacArthur Causeway and the turquoise Biscayne Bay are on display from the highest mobile vantage point in the city.

If you're near the financial district around Brickell, wander through the maze of one of the country's largest concrete jungles. Stand beneath the Southeast Financial Center's zigzag cubic roof that hovers hundreds of feet above the ground. A few stops up the line, get off at Bayside. Visit the Perez Art Museum (see p. 92) and the adjacent Frost Museum of Science right next to the Museum Park stop. Catch a show at the New World School of the Arts, alma mater of *It's Always Sunny in Philadelphia's* Glenn Howerton.

At night, the silhouette of a 35-story-tall burlesque performer dances on the broad side of the InterContinental Hotel (see p. 108) just outside the Bayfront Park stop, and Brickell's bar and club scene booms with Blackbird Ordinary, a bar-club hybrid mainstay, just two blocks from the Eighth Street station.

Address Downtown Miami; see map of stations at www.miamidade.gov/transit/metromover-stations.asp | Hours Daily 5am–midnight | Tip The Metromover happens to connect to Miami's Metrorail, which services the airport. If you need to get to Downtown from the airport and don't want to fight the traffic, this is the way to go.

66__Miami Auto Museum

The city's grandest carport

Sun and fun be damned, motorheads have an indoor, air-conditioned haven in North Miami, thanks to New York real-estate developer Michael Dezer. The man who developed Trump Towers and Trump Grande Ocean Resort and Residences also has an undying passion for automobiles. Hidden among the storage facilities and concrete manufacturers that populate much of the neighborhood, you will find his hobby's home, at the Miami Auto Museum, which features a cross section of the world's coolest cars.

There is something for everyone at Dezer's motor palace. Start off in the classics wing, where the collection of wheeled vehicles is designed to take you on a trip through automotive history. The sharp fins of old Cadillacs are sandwiched between an army jeep from World War II and an old French Peugeot. Along a snaking pathway, the evolution of two-wheeled transportation, from penny-farthings to Vespa scooters, is on display.

The Hollywood wing is by far the most popular. Batmobiles driven by dark knights ranging from Adam West to Michael Keaton line the entryway to the masses of motorized movie memorabilia. See the magical car from *Chitty Chitty Bang Bang's* final landing spot, almost 50 years after huffing and puffing through Vulgaria. Lean in and take a look at the flux capacitor of Marty McFly's DeLorean, fresh out of plutonium fuel. Get up close to Scooby Doo's Mystery Machine, the Dukes' General Lee, the Ghostbusters' Ecto-1, and John Travolta's Grease Lightning.

The crown jewel of the Miami Auto Museum, however, is the James Bond display. Sleek black tiles on the floor and bright white lights above perfectly set the stage for the BMW from *Tomorrow Never Dies*, the Aston Martin from *Goldfinger*, the gun-turreted Land Rover from *Skyfall*, and the rest of 007's cars, boats, airplanes, and snowmobiles, all polished to a high shine.

Address 2000 NE 146th Street, Miami, FL 33181, +1 305.354.7680, www.dezercollection.com | Hours Daily 10am–6pm | Tip Shed your inhibitions and go skinny-dipping at Haulover's nude beach (10800 Collins Ave, Miami Beach).

67_Miami Catamarans

Sailing solace

The warm blue waters of Biscayne Bay are Miami's aquatic playground. Mega-yachts, sailboats, powerboats, and Jet Skis speed along, passing under causeways to and from the Atlantic Ocean. Boats pull water-skiers, who cross, flip, and jump the wakes; parasailers, who are suspended above the water by their vibrant chutes; and tubers, who plow through the swells. A ride on a catamaran combines the best of all worlds, just as thrilling as it is relaxing.

A catamaran harnesses the wind for locomotion in the same way other sailboats do, although its two narrow pontoon hulls and trampoline deck make it much faster than a traditional sailboat. If it's a blustery day, these vessels can glide through the waves easily in excess of 20 miles per hour.

Experienced sailors tuck their feet into straps on the trampoline, pull the sail in tight to catch more of the wind, and fly a hull – letting one pontoon rise out of the water as they continue to sail at an angle between 45 and nearly 90 degrees; a heart-pounding ride that flirts with capsizing at any moment as they use their bodies as ballast to weigh the high side down.

For the more faint of heart, keeping both pontoons in the water offers a uniquely intimate experience with Biscayne Bay. It's fast enough to get you to your destination in a timely fashion, but slow enough to let you absorb the panoramic views from Brickell's towering skyline to Stiltsville's floating houses. Lie prone on the trampoline and skim above the water, facing the field of blue head-on. Water occasionally splashes up from beneath the mesh platform, offering a cool, refreshing reminder of how close you are to the sea below. Look up and see the catamaran's brilliant sail cut through the wind like a knife, piloting you through the bay and into the ocean. A rainbow of colors adorns the towering sail that dwarfs the platform underneath, traversing the waters in swift silence.

Address 3301 Rickenbacker Causeway, Miami, FL 33149, +1 305.345.4104, www.miamicatamarans.com | Hours Daily 10am–7:30pm | Tip If you're into aquatic life, head to the Miami Seaquarium (4400 Rickenbacker Causeway), a Miami institution since 1955. Manatees, orcas, dolphins, and other sea creatures call the Seaquarium home.

68 Miami Circle

Ancient ruins in a modern jungle

Downtown, where the Miami River meets Biscayne Bay, surrounded by multimillion-dollar apartments, 500-foot-high office buildings, and five-star restaurants, sits an ancient settlement, as undisturbed as it was millennia ago.

The Miami Circle is the only known prehistoric cut-in-rock structure in eastern North America to date. Anywhere from 1000 to 2000 years ago, the Tequesta tribe, which had inhabited South Florida since the 3rd century BCE, constructed a perfect circle that archaeologists believe was the foundation of a "council house." The structure appeared to be oriented to the cardinal directions and possibly the stars, much in the way the famous henges of Britain were. The Tequesta's central city was believed to be at the mouth of the Miami River, where the circle is situated.

After the apartment complex at 401 Brickell Avenue was torn down in 1998, the prehistoric structure was discovered. Upon excavation, researchers found a number of post holes dug into the oolitic limestone foundation arranged in a perfect circle measuring 38 feet in diameter. Some scientists believe the holes were made for stilts that held up a greater structure, perhaps of a ceremonial or religious nature. Artifacts, such as a shark skeleton buried in east-west alignment, a complete sea-turtle carapace, basalt axes, and human teeth, were also found at the site.

The empty air above Miami Circle creates a noticeable gap in the Downtown skyline. The Icon Brickell, the neighboring condominium supported by faux Easter Island heads, towers above the site, which is just as old, if not older, than the actual moai on Easter Island. To the north, boats pass under the Brickell Avenue bridge in the shadows of some of Miami's tallest buildings. To the south, the heart of Downtown pulses. To the east, Biscayne Bay's waters wash up to the Tequesta settlement as it did thousands of years ago.

Address 401 Brickell Avenue Miami, FL 33131 | Tip Oddly enough, Sun Life Stadium (347 Don Shula Dr) in Miami Gardens was built on an ancient Tequesta burial ground. As the home field for both the Miami Hurricanes and Miami Dolphins, one might seriously consider the legitimacy of poltergeists after seeing either of these teams struggle to become the successes they once were.

69 Miami Club Rum

South Beach's sustenance

The city that bridges the cultural gap between the Americas drowns in cocktails and frozen drinks to the delight of both tourists and locals. Vodka, gin, and whiskey flow freely at the innumerable bars and nightclubs from South Beach to Doral, but of all libations, rum is the most culturally pervasive. For hundreds of years, Cuba and other Latin American countries forged strong economic ties with the States by way of the rum trade and manufacturing.

Matthew Malone's in-laws had made rum for five generations in Mayaguez, Puerto Rico. In 2012, he decided to continue the tradition. "I had to keep this going for my children," Malone said about hatching the idea for Miami Club Rum, the city's first rum distillery.

In the bowels of the Wynwood distillery, Malone incorporates his family's age-old secret rum recipes. First, the four fermentation tanks, named Greta, Eva, Margaret, and Rock Hudson, are filled with yeast and local sugarcane. Then, the "sugarcane wine" is moved to the old still, affectionately called Sugar Lips, and heated. The alcoholic vapors boil up through the metal pipe, condense, and are collected in three parts. The "head" and "tail" are the inferior by-products, and are either recycled for further distillation or used as cleaning agents. The remaining *corazon* is placed in "music infused" aging tanks. During the three months the rum is aged in these vats, salsa and merengue tunes are played through vintage Bose 901 speakers. According to Malone, the music is a sonic tool that "creates a physical and metaphysical impression upon the spirits," whose vibrations "release deep flavors from within the wood."

A key ingredient to any Cuba Libre, this coconut-filtered crystal clear libation is slowly taking over South Beach with its warm, buttery palate and a smooth finish that defies its 84 proof. Crack open a bottle and let the tunes flow.

Address 10 NW 24th Street, Miami, FL 33127, +1 844.642.2582,
www.miamiclubrum.com | Hours Tours and tastings by appointment only | Tip If you're in
Miami in mid- to late April, check out the Rum Renaissance Festival at the Miami Airport
Convention Center (711 NW 72nd Ave), where you can sample hundreds of different rums
from international distilleries.

70__Miami Jai-Alai
The "world's fastest game"

Shouting players behind a mesh partition create visual art out of pure physical skill; the *pelota* (a small leather ball) is launched from the player's hooked wicker *cesta* (a handheld banana-shaped basket) at incredible speed and ricochets off the front wall. The eight players on the floor duck, dodge, and climb the surrounding walls to grab the next shot without getting beaned by the ball or slammed by another player. As the match progresses, the number of players in the *fronton* (court) dwindles until a player or team gets their "Spectacular Seven" points.

Jai alai was once the pounding heart of Miami's sports and gambling scene. The first *fronton* in Florida opened on the site of the Hialeah racetrack in 1924, which was moved to the current Miami Jai-Alai two years later. In the 1960s and 1970s, people flocked to Miami Jai-Alai to spend an evening drinking, gambling, and getting lost in the haze of the smoke-filled stands to watch the "world's fastest game." In its heyday, the thundering boom of the *pelota* smashing against the wall was inaudible, drowned out by the noise of the crowd shouting over wins and losses. Turnouts then regularly exceeded 10,000, making it hard to get a good seat. Now, attendance averages a hundred or two – on a good day.

Over the years, the popularity of football in Miami overtook jai alai as the city's premier sporting attraction. The Dolphins put themselves on the map after their 1972 undefeated season, and the University of Miami Hurricanes began their rise to national prominence in the early 1980s.

Today, the major "action" at Miami Jai-Alai is at the casino, not the *fronton*. For those watching the game, however, the drama on the floor is no less charged now than it was 50 years ago. Competitors still risk injury every time the *pelota* is fired. Sitting in the mostly empty stands, an eerie but exciting feeling washes over you, as if the rapid-fire game on display is being played all for you.

Address 3500 NW 37th Avenue, Miami, FL 33142, +1 305.633.6400, www.casinomiamijaialai.com | Hours Games start at 1pm on Sun and noon on Mon and Wed–Fri (closed on Tue) | Tip This neighborhood isn't the safest in the city, so best to visit during the daytime.

71 Miami Marine Stadium

Beautiful urban blight

In a run-down parking lot off Rickenbacker Causeway sits an abandoned megalith. Miami Marine Stadium is the unkempt concrete canvas that welcomes visitors to Virginia Key.

Marine Stadium was a concert and event venue overlooking the pristine waters of Biscayne Bay. Its happenings ranged from boat shows to presidential campaign rallies; from the Florida Philharmonic to the all-too-regular Jimmy Buffet concert. As time wore on, however, the stadium became increasingly neglected. In 1992, the city claimed that Hurricane Andrew caused millions of dollars in damage, forcing them to close the structure. In the 15 or so years that followed, vandals and street artists had their way with the stadium. And as its walls became increasingly stratified with layers of spray paint, its renaissance began.

The vandalized facades of ticket booths and concession stands offer a graffitied appetizer for what lies beyond the tunnels that lead to the grandstand. At the base of the bleachers, the water laps up against the abandoned slip. Everywhere else, stunning, spray-painted murals overrun every available surface. Memorials, protests, obscenities, and mindless doodles juxtapose themselves, creating a chaotic, stunning collage. The allure lies not only in the sheer amount of graffiti, but in the diversity and fluidity of the tags as a whole. The entire structure has become an interactive piece of art. Distinguished street artists create elaborate murals capturing the social conditions of Miami, but amateurs deface them before they're even dry; the only permanence is the stadium's existence.

It's now a fitting metaphor for the city's rebirth. Once a clean-cut destination for a Saturday boat race with the family, Marine Stadium had devolved into a purposeless spectator of the city's watershed years. And much like the city, the stadium has been totally reenergized by Miami's youth and art scene.

Address 3501 Rickenbacker Causeway, Key Biscayne, FL 33149 | Hours Not open to the public | Tip Northwest of the stadium, at the western terminus of the Rickenbacker Causeway's high bridge, is a quaint little park you can drive into for a great view of Miami's downtown skyline. There's usually a food cart there selling warm arepas and cold bottles of water.

72 Mitzi's Memorial

R.I.P. Flipper

A gray flash beneath the water catches the attention of the audience. Suddenly surfacing, the smiling dolphin puffs through its blowhole and emits a squeaky, high-pitched tone before plunging back underwater. Will it shoot up from beneath and do an aerial somersault? Will it rise up on its tail and propel itself across the lagoon? The archetypal sea mammal that burned these maneuvers into the minds of millions around the globe once resided here on Grassy Key. Mitzi, better known as Flipper, the world's most famous bottlenose dolphin, spent her final days at what is now the Dolphin Research Center.

The facility was originally founded in 1958 as Santini's Porpoise School. Mitzi, who was Milton Santini's first pupil, launched the training center to national prominence after her heartwarming debut performance in *Flipper* in 1963 at the tender age of five. In the film, Flipper is accidentally speared by a fisherman and rescued by Sandy Ricks, played by actor Luke Halpin. As an expression of her gratitude, Flipper takes a liking to young Sandy and soon becomes his best friend and protector. If sharks are afoot, Flipper chases them away. If Sandy and his pals want a show, Flipper gladly obliges them.

On the heels of *Flipper's* success, visitors came to Santini's to "ride" Mitzi or have her tug them along on a small boat. She retired from her movie career after the 1964 sequel, *Flipper's New Adventure*. In 1972, Mitzi passed away from a heart attack at the age of 14 and a memorial was erected here in her honor.

Since 1984, the Dolphin Research Center has been devoted to creating a wholesome environment for both its human visitors and sea-mammal residents, offering the best care and rehabilitation for dolphins and seals deemed unfit to live in the wild, while providing a rich educational experience for curious guests. For the existence and continuous growth of the DRC, we have Mitzi to thank.

Address 58901 Overseas Highway, Grassy Key, FL 33050, +1 305.289.1121, www.dolphins.org | Hours Daily 9am–4:30pm | Tip Visit the nearby Keys Cable Park (59300 Overseas Hwy) in Marathon to go wakeboarding. Whip and flip on a rentable wakeboard, the hipper alternative to waterskiing. Lessons are available for beginners.

73 Monkey Jungle

Catching up with your ancestors

Unlike most zoos, Monkey Jungle is where the primates roam free and watch caged humans move through their environment.

In the early 1930s, animal behaviorist Joseph DuMond let loose a small group of Southeast Asian crab-eating macaques into this hammock in western Dade County to observe them in a simulated natural habitat. In the 80 years that followed, Monkey Jungle grew into a rich preserve that includes a lush Amazonian rain forest. Today, hundreds of monkeys, including many descendants of the original group brought over by DuMond, call the park home.

Visitors move through wire mesh tunnels while macaques and squirrel monkeys, meandering above, politely reach down and shake chains dangling from the ceiling beneath them for food. You can drop some raisins in the bowl at the end of a chain, and the monkey will swiftly reel it in. Mimicking their elders' techniques for acquiring sweets, adorable infant monkeys follow suit. If a stray baby approaches with an outstretched hand, you can sneak a little something through the grating and watch him enjoy it right in front of you.

Other species, like the technicolor-faced mandrills and the white-handed gibbons, are segregated to keep interspecies violence from erupting. May, the orangutan, greets onlookers from her grotto by clapping her hands and blowing kisses. King, the silverback gorilla, and 45-year-old lord of Monkey Jungle, downs a bottle of iced tea, tosses the empty bottle in a recycling bin, then stands and beats his chest, full of pride.

In 1992, Monkey Jungle was ravaged by Hurricane Andrew. Packs of monkeys roamed the rural Redlands southwest of Miami's city center, fending for themselves in the rubble left by the storm's wake. Restoration was an easy cause for South Floridians to rally behind – it's been a beloved institution for generations – and since then, the park has returned to its original fullness.

Address 14805 Southwest 216th Street, Miami, FL 33170, +1 305.235.1611, www.monkeyjungle.com | Hours Daily 9:30am–5pm (ticket office closes at 4pm) | Tip This area is about as remote as it gets in Miami-Dade County. With that comes reduced gas prices, so if your car needs refueling, this is the place to do it.

74 National Key Deer Refuge

Bambi's baby brothers and sisters

The Florida Keys are home to a diverse wildlife population. There is marine life aplenty – tarpon, dolphin, sharks, sea turtles, even the stray alligator or two, not to mention sand skinks and wood storks that have trickled their way south. The Keys have their share of land mammals, too, including marsh rabbits and the endangered Key Largo woodrat, which looks like a cross between a sewer rat and a gerbil. But the region's most unique critter is the Key deer. The smallest species of deer in North America (and smallest species of white-tailed deer in the world) finds its only home on Big Pine Key.

The island is so well populated by these pint-sized deer that its main thoroughfare outside of Overseas Highway is named Key Deer Boulevard; heading toward the northern end of Big Pine Key, you'll see deer crossing signs all along the roadside. The deer population here is so dense, they frequently pop out from the surrounding brush, so it's absolutely necessary to drive slowly to avoid a collision. The farther north you go, the more alert you need to be, as the deer become increasingly abundant.

If you happen to spot some deer on the side of the road, don't hesitate to pull over and check them out. They're roughly the size of medium to large dogs, weighing 60 pounds and standing about two feet tall on average. Aside from their diminutive size, their temperament is also different from that of other deer species. Due to their close living proximity to humans, Key deer are generally more curious and friendly. In most cases, if you stand near one, they will approach you without much hesitation, most likely in search of food. Feeding them is unlawful, but petting them is not.

As ubiquitous as they may seem, do not be fooled; they are as endangered as they are adorable. There are less than one thousand of these big-eyed, knock-kneed animals in the world, and they all live here.

Address Visitor Center, 179 Key Deer Boulevard, Big Pine Key, FL 33043, +1 305.872.0774, www.fws.gov/nationalkeydeer | Hours Mon–Fri 9am–4pm, Sat–Sun 10am–3pm | Tip Recapture your youth while enjoying the fruits of adulthood at Boondock's (27205 Overseas Hwy) in Ramrod Key, just west of Big Pine Key. Grab a beer from the bar and play a round or two of mini-golf.

75__News Cafe

People-watching paradise

In the heart of the Art Deco District, News Cafe is just steps from Lummus Park to the east and the Colony Hotel to the south. Under the shade of its dark green awning, the open-air eatery buzzes with crowds of people from every walk of South Beach society – residents, partyers, and tourists – all looking to grab a quick bite. The drone of simultaneous conversations in English, Spanish, French, Russian, Chinese, Swedish; the clinking of glasses; and occasional blare of a taxicab's horn sets the scene from sunset to sunset. But it's not the food that should lure you to one of the cafe's outdoor tables; it's the promise of some good old-fashioned people-watching. Grab a *Miami Herald*, pull up a chair, order a coffee, and settle in to watch the most entertaining show on Miami Beach. As hordes of South Beachers pass by in their unadulterated glory, a corner table outside News Cafe is simply the best seat in the house.

Ocean Drive is Miami's catwalk. Many that roam this stretch seem more like they're straight out of central casting than actual people. Flip to the sports section of the paper while ogling the city's most interesting characters, from the underdressed to the overdressed, the bedazzled to the bedraggled, the leather-skinned to the dressed-like-twins, the fanny packers to the fashion elite. Enjoy a sip of coffee while you covertly gaze at the group of bleached-blonde Scandinavian women all sporting identical rhinestone-encrusted Yankees hats. Rest your mug, pretend to turn to the front page, and peer at the drunken underage couple unapologetically stumbling through the intersection, almost becoming a news story in themselves as they narrowly avoid oncoming traffic. Forget about being inconspicuous and blatantly stare at the bikini-clad fire-breathing juggler riding a unicycle in the middle of traffic (seriously), all from your curbside perch.

But just remember: if you can see them, they can see you …

Address 800 Ocean Drive, Miami Beach, FL 33139, +1 305.538.6397, www.newscafe.com | Hours 24 hours a day | Tip Walk south on Ocean Drive and see many of Miami's famed Art Deco hotels up close. The Starlite, Boulevard, and Colony hotels are situated, one after another, just across the street from News Cafe.

76__O Cinema
Popcorn and circumstance

In a neighborhood overflowing with public art, it's a little tougher to find a place where the art is inside the building, rather than on it. Nestled between a small film-production warehouse, and an even smaller single-family home, is O Cinema.

The venue maintains a quiet presence in a neighborhood that prides itself on being loud. The exterior's garage door is graffitied over; it's a necessary homage to the community it resides in. The theater's immediate interior is bare bones, with stark black walls and plain white floors. An unadorned concession counter, with a wall of stacked crates filled with soft drinks in plain sight, greets guests immediately as they walk through the front door. Vegan muffins, cookies, and granola bars take the place of the standard Sno-Caps and gummy bears. That unmistakable popcorn smell radiates from the tiny popcorn machine sitting at the edge of the counter and fills the lobby, as proper movie-house protocol calls for.

The corner areas of the lobby walls are reserved for displaying the work of local artists. In the hallway that leads to the rear of the theater, you'll find another impromptu gallery, about the size of a water closet. In the next room over, there's a compact reading space with a quirky selection of titles, ranging from picture books documenting the Cuban Revolution to Judy Blume's *Superfudge* to Kafka's *The Metamorphosis*.

The curation of films is equally eclectic, much like the Thalia or Film Forum programs in New York City during the 1980s. Screenings might include Charlie Chaplin's *Gold Rush* one week and the eighties kid classic *Land Before Time* the next. O Cinema is the place to go to catch the Oscar-nominated shorts and other independent features and documentaries you won't find in the mainstream multiplexes. It's unique in its cultivation of film, art, and literature, all under one roof.

Address 90 NW 29th Street, Miami, FL 33127, +1 305.571.9970, www.o-cinema.org | Hours Opens 1 hour before the day's first film (check website for showtimes) | Tip After catching a movie at O Cinema, head down to the Electric Pickle (2826 N Miami Ave) for a nightcap. The Wynwood bar and music club describes itself as a "liquor-fueled love machine."

77__Ochopee Post Office

Littlest house on the prairie

One of the most remote areas of Florida clings to civilization by a thread. At the southwest corner of the Big Cypress National Preserve, in the middle of Collier County, a one-room building stands alone on the side of the Tamiami Trail. An American flag flutters in the hot breeze that rolls through the Everglades, shading a small white shack with a metal awning, a historical plaque, and a couple of blue mailboxes. Once a tool shed, the country's smallest post office, or perhaps America's largest mailbox, serves the unincorporated community of Ochopee, a town whose human population is outnumbered by alligators.

Looking out from the post office, saw-grass prairies and marshy wetlands extend in every direction as far as the eye can see; it's no secret that Ochopee's roots are steeped in agriculture. In the late 1920s, entrepreneur James Gaunt bought 250 of these untamed acres lying along the newly paved Tamiami Trail for tomato farming. He, his family, and his employees lived in army surplus tents during the first months of his operation, fighting daily battles against the intense heat and pesky insects of the Everglades. A permanent settlement was soon built, and as Gaunt's enterprise continued to grow, a post office was built into his newly constructed company store.

The post office at Gaunt's farm held firm in Ochopee until 1953, when a blaze that started in the boardinghouse spread and burned the post office, among other structures, to the ground. Fortunately, the postmaster had the wherewithal to salvage most of the documents inside. Unfortunately, when the mail arrived the next day, there was no place to put it. The postmaster improvised and decided to use the small shed that housed irrigation equipment as a makeshift depot. For 60 years and counting, the tiny eight by seven-foot shack has remained Ochopee's post office.

Address 38000 Tamiami Trail E, Ochopee, FL 34141 | Hours Mon–Fri 8am–10am, noon–4pm, Sat 10am–11:30am | Tip Check out the old Monroe Station (50910 Tamiami Trail E), a former roadside stop for weary travelers in the 1920s, at the junction of Tamiami Trail and Loop Rd. The old wooden building is dilapidated and completely boarded up, but still standing after weathering multiple hurricanes.

78_ Old Cutler Road

Banyan-covered bliss

Stretching from Coral Gables to Cutler Bay, in the southwest section of town, Old Cutler Road provides lushly shaded relief from Miami's drab, congested thoroughfares. A blessing in the summer months, banyan and ficus trees canopy the drive, cooling and filtering the sun's harsh rays. Camouflaged by the dripping foliage are stunning homes in nearly every style: from old ivy-covered Italian villas featuring wrought-iron gates and clay tile roofs, to sleek white monoliths with thick, aquamarine-colored windows. Maseratis and Ferraris adorn many driveways.

Signs along the side of the road ask that you keep driving instead of pulling over to admire the beauty. Despite this command to keep traffic flowing, you won't be able to resist stopping for a better look every now and then. Fortunately, there are continuous bike paths and sidewalks, and if you have the time to cycle Old Cutler, you won't regret it.

The road itself is named after the now-defunct farming town of Cutler, which owes its name to Dr. William Cutler, a Massachusetts doctor who fell in love with the area in the 19th century. The winding road – the first to connect Coconut Grove to the town of Cutler – followed a natural limestone ridge along Biscayne Bay. Over time, the road was continuously widened, first to accommodate wagons and, eventually, cars. Despite the numerous modifications, Old Cutler's atmosphere has remained virtually the same.

Some of the most picturesque parks and gardens in Miami are situated along this stretch of asphalt. The calm waters of Matheson Hammock (see p. 132) gently lap against its shoreline. The majestic Deering Estate (see p. 66) towers in the distance. The colorful Fairchild Tropical Gardens (see p. 208) lures visitors like their hibiscus flowers lure the bumblebees. The most dramatic views, luxurious homes, and densest awning of branches can be seen from Fairchild to the traffic circle at Cocoplum.

Address Old Cutler runs from Cocoplum Circle in Coral Gables down to SW 216th Street in Cutler Bay | **Tip** Just north of where Old Cutler begins, a super-exclusive garden estate is tucked away in the middle of Coral Gables. The Kampong (4013 South Douglas Rd, Miami), former home of botanist David Fairchild, is open to the public by appointment only.

79 __ Old Planetarium

Retro planetary retrograde

The Miami planetarium opened in 1966 and for almost half a century, the giant golden igloo on the northeast edge of Coconut Grove welcomed generations of school-age kids to reach for the stars. As time went by, the surrounding community became swept up in movements of the sixties and seventies, like legalizing marijuana and gay rights. But the planetarium remained steadfastly and charmingly rooted in the past.

Up until its final days, the planetarium took visitors on a trip into space as well as back in time. The massive black globe in the lobby boasted a map from the old Pan Am terminal down the street, which included countries like Siam and Rhodesia. A retro "Planetarium in use" sign flashed above old wooden double doors like the "Applause" sign on the set of Johnny Carson's *Tonight Show*.

Inside the theater, at the center of it all, sat the Spitz Model B Space Transit Projector. A round, menacing steel beast of a star simulator, the once cutting-edge machine long outlived its life expectancy of 20 years. In fact, the projector was so advanced for its time that it was once used to train astronauts by simulating a flight to the moon. The celestial show cast onto the ceiling was compelling enough to make anyone a sci-fi nerd. Even more mesmerizing was watching the Spitz projector gyrate, spin, and turn upside down, as lights would flash in and around its innumerable tiny pinholes, mirrors, and miniature lenses.

The projector shone one last time on August 30th, 2015. In a bittersweet transition, the beloved landmark was shuttered to make way for a shiny modernized planetarium at the newly incorporated Museum Park, right next to the Perez Art Museum. While the projector will be on display as an exhibit in its new digs just 20 minutes up the road, the glittering celestial shell of the old planetarium still stands as an enduring reminder of a bygone era.

Address 3280 South Miami Avenue, Miami, FL 33129, +1 305.646.4269, www.miamisci.org | Hours Viewable from the outside; open for special events (check website) | Tip Grab a meal at Green Street Café (3468 Main Hwy), a Coconut Grove institution. Founded in the early 1990s, Green Street offers modern European fare, from breakfast through dinner.

80_ Oleta River State Park
Row into the city

Amid the strip malls and white-sand beaches of North Miami is a lush river valley shrouded by mangroves. Oleta River State Park, where a remnant of untouched Everglades spills into Biscayne Bay, is where Miamians go for a taste of nature in the middle of the city. To the northeast, the high-rise condominiums and hotels of Sunny Isles Beach loom; to the south are the ritzy shops of Bal Harbour. Just across the bay, nude beachgoers and kite flyers populate both sides of Haulover Park. Sprawled across 1,000 acres of wilderness, this urban oasis offers a wealth of recreational diversions. Sunbathe in a sandy cove, go for a hike through the thick tropical brush, bike the magnificent nature trails shaded by Australian Pines, or best of all, row your kayak along the Oleta River into northern Biscayne Bay.

The Oleta River has never been dredged or channeled to accommodate boats or commerce, making it the only natural river in Dade County. Its abundance of saw grass and cattails is an ironic contrast to the surrounding metropolis. Rent a canoe, kayak, or paddleboard to fully experience the waterways that snake their way through mangrove tunnels. Start from the northern end of the park and row southward. The dense thickets in narrow, winding creeks gradually open up; dolphins may appear in the warm, translucent waters underneath you while Miami's skyline is visible beyond the treetops.

Oleta River Park is a picturesque escape from city life, but still within walking distance. Small boats and bicycles are the only traffic here. Enjoy a picnic in one of the park's pavilions. Didn't bring enough food? Zip over to the Publix supermarket on Collins Avenue, just a 10-minute drive away. Or, for a fraction of what it would cost to stay one night at the Fontainebleau, spend a few nights in a primitive but air-conditioned log cabin. You'll almost forget you're in the midst of one of the most cosmopolitan cities in the world.

Address 3400 NE 163rd Street, North Miami, FL 33181, +1 305.919.1846, www.floridastateparks.org/park/Oleta-River | Hours Daily 8am–sunset | Tip Every full moon, at North Shore Open Space Park in North Beach (A1A and 85th St), a giant drum circle forms to honor the lunar event.

81 Orion Herbs

Miami's medicine man

On the second floor of the old Giller Building, right off the Julia Tuttle Causeway, Orion Nevel runs Miami Beach's holistic haven, its alternative ashram. Shelves brimming with bottles of capsules and elixirs encase the tiny office space. Stressed out? Ask for a lavender-oil tincture. Have a stomachache? Ask for the green superfood supplement. Still not sure what you need? Ask Orion.

In 1982, Daniel Atchison-Nevel and his wife, Jane, founded one of the country's first comprehensive holistic health centers, in Miami Beach. The center gathered dozens of health care providers, from medical doctors to energy healers, into one practice, and also featured a diagnostic facility that employed both conventional and cutting-edge technologies. In this setting, established by his parents, Orion, the shaman of Miami Beach, learned his trade.

The unfamiliar aroma of valerian, anise, echinacea, triphala, and albizzia bark perfumes the corridor leading to Orion's herbal pharmacy. Through the creaky wooden door and into the dark vestibule, Orion's shop is directly to your left. Inside, he waits with natural remedies on hand for almost any ailment, from heartburn to headaches, anxiety to fatigue, colds and flus to scrapes and burns.

Orion is diligent about verifying the sourcing and quality of all the herbs and ingredients he uses. He's even traveled to their countries of origin to meet the growers and producers in person. He runs the products he sells through a battery of tests and analyses to confirm their efficacy. Vendors are carefully vetted by a board of practitioners. New products are tailored to each individual patient, based on how they respond to certain herbs that have been prescribed for them. If many patients react well to a certain supplement, Orion preps the remedies in-house and markets them under his label, Orion Herbs.

Address 975 Arthur Godfrey Road, Suite 211, Miami Beach, FL 33140, +1 305.672.3901, www.orionherbs.com | Hours Mon, Wed, and Fri 8:30am–6:30pm, Tue and Thu 10am–4pm | Tip Head east on Arthur Godfrey to Capri (726 Arthur Godfrey Rd), a kosher, Italian-Japanese fusion restaurant. Have tuna tataki for an appetizer and roasted pear salad as an entree.

82 Panther Coffee

You're not in Starbucks anymore

Within Wynwood's technicolor concrete jungle sits the hub of daytime socializing. Panther Coffee is where the bustling art and design district gets its buzz. Hipsters unite in this repurposed storage facility – one of many in the neighborhood – awash with thick-framed glasses, Macbooks, tattered shirts, and skinny jeans.

The facade used to sport an Escher-esque green-and-red three-dimensional checkerboard, but after vandals relentlessly tagged the mural, Panther's frontage was painted completely black. Ironically, the monochromatic exterior makes it stand out amid Wynwood's brightly painted buildings and walls. But what truly sets Panther apart is their otherworldly coffee. Priding itself on diligent sourcing and quality, Panther buys its beans in small batches in the raw, then roasts and grinds in-house.

Humanity is tightly packed into this small, raucous caffeine cloister. The line to place an order snakes its way through the tiny room. If you haven't figured out what you want by the time you reach the front of the line, you'll have to read the small clipboard menu at the counter quickly to keep both the human traffic and drinks flowing. You'll see selections from across the globe, and you can't go wrong with any of them. Go ahead and blurt out the first thing that sounds good, hand the nice barista your payment, and wait with the rest of your comrades-in-coffee, huddled around the vintage bean roaster on display at the back of the shop, until you hear your name being shouted across the room.

With seats nearly impossible to find inside, brave the heat and humidity and enjoy your espresso drink on the front patio. Panther's courtyard, furnished with concrete benches and tables, has become a breeding ground for networking and creative collaborations. Relax and watch the ideas hatch over a steaming cappuccino made from scratch.

Address 2390 NW 2nd Avenue, Miami, FL 33127, +1 305.677.3952, www.panthercoffee.com | Hours Mon–Sat 7am–9pm, Sun 8am–9pm | Tip A short walk east on NW 24th St will bring you to Gramps (176 NW 24th St), a tavern advertising "Air Conditioning, Cold Beer, and Cocktails" on the front of the building.

83 Perky's Bat Tower

Mosquito mishap

In the dead heat of a South Floridian summer, the mosquito population can seem insufferable; the buzzing blood-hungry insects breed profusely in the still, shallow waters that cover the Everglades and surround the Keys. At nearly every outdoor establishment, from restaurants to campgrounds, the smell of bug spray and burning citronella candles permeates the air. Yet, as much of an annoyance as today's mosquitoes are, their impact was immeasurably worse before the mass use of pesticides.

It is said that in pre-pesticide times, mosquitoes would sometimes form in clouds so thick that residents of the Keys would breathe them in by the mouthful. It was once even reported that over 350,000 mosquitoes were caught overnight in just one trap.

During the land boom of the 1920s, real-estate developer R. C. Perky bought property in the Keys, including acreage on Sugarloaf Key. Perky was well aware of the mosquito problem that bedeviled the Keys, and was intent on combatting it. After reading a book called *Bats, Mosquitoes, and Dollars*, Perky hired Fred Johnson, a sponge cultivator from Key West, to build him a tower to house bats – nature's mosquito predators. The tower was based on the design described in the book, authored by a Texan named Dr. Charles Campbell – the inventor of the bat-roost. Perky followed the guidelines outlined by Dr. Campbell and imported hundreds of bats from Cuba and Texas to nest in the 30-foot tall wood-shingled tower. Perky even brought in sex-scented bat droppings, at significant expense, to attract the web-winged creatures to the tower. Unfortunately for Perky, the bats flew out the first night and never returned.

Today, on the dilapidated, unmarked Bat Tower Road, the tower still stands on Sugarloaf Key as it did in 1929. Its only resident is an osprey, whose nest is perched atop what is now the Florida Keys' most formidable birdhouse.

Address 4 Bat Tower Road, Monroe County, FL 33042 | Tip While you're in Sugarloaf Key, why not go skydiving? Head to Skydive Key West (5 Bat Tower Rd) and parachute thousands of feet down to the sandy floor below.

84__Pinecrest Gardens

Bye bye birdies

Years ago, entering this lush, green environment was near deafening. The threshold, shaded by a cluster of banyan trees, was teeming with blue and scarlet macaws resting on their perches, squawking at visitors for a pittance of sunflower seeds. Beyond the welcoming chorus of macaws was Pinky, a 60-year-old cockatoo, who rode a small bicycle on a highwire for delighted audiences. The fauna ran the show at the old Parrot Jungle. The flora provided a nice but often overlooked backdrop.

Once the animals were relocated to a new home on Watson Island in 2003, the exquisite tropical garden took center stage. Blooming orchids seemed to explode. The intricate ficus canopies that shaded the entire park came into focus, and old wooden bridges over trickling, fern-encased coral creeks emerged from the background.

The original iconic sign that greeted visitors looks nearly the same today, except the white letters that once spelled "Parrot Jungle" now say "Pinecrest Gardens," and the two painted macaws have been replaced by a just-as-tremendous hibiscus flower. The amphitheater still exists, as do the cavernous, ivy-clad tunnels that lace its perimeter. The addition of a petting zoo and playground makes for a child-friendly atmosphere. Check in with the events calendar on the gardens' website for jazz performances, orchid club functions, and other events. Botanical tours are available by appointment, and on Family Movie Nights, there are guided flashlight tours.

Overall, the grounds have taken an elegant step forward from the aviary they once were. The crushed tile mosaic walkways and coral fences swirl up to the observation deck and around the deep gully that provides a home for the few creatures that come and go as they please. Fallen trees from past hurricanes are grown over, offering a beautiful metaphor for what the park was and what it has become.

Address 11000 S Red Road, Miami, FL 33156, +1 305.669.6990, www.pinecrest-fl.gov/index.aspx?page=34 | Hours Fall and winter: Mon–Fri 10am–5pm, Sat and Sun 9am–5pm; spring and summer: Mon–Fri 10am–6pm, Sat and Sun 9am–6pm | Tip Every Sunday, Pinecrest Gardens hosts a bustling farmers market – a favorite among locals.

85 Rickenbacker Causeway

Feel the burn

Miami's a flat city, with an average elevation of six feet above sea level. The turquoise ocean waters roll up onto the sand, blown by the wind into parking lots and onto the streets. In the dog days of summer, which generally run from late April to early November, the heat and humidity thickens the air from Sunny Isles Beach all the way down to Key West. The occasional ocean breeze is a godsend, a divine gift of fleeting temperate relief that reminds you that these oppressive conditions aren't permanent. But even on the stickiest of days, a quick jog on the Rickenbacker Causeway serves as a healthful, and even cool, consolation.

As the sole gateway to Key Biscayne since 1947, the Rickenbacker Causeway was a drawbridge for the first 40 years of its existence. Named after Eddie Rickenbacker, famed war hero and then president of the Miami-based Eastern Airlines, the causeway provided easy access to some of Miami's best beaches. In 1980, with the causeway's popularity increasing, the high-rise bridge that stands today was erected.

Unlike the MacArthur and Julia Tuttle Causeways, Rickenbacker's traffic is relatively light. But the cool winds that blow in from Biscayne Bay to the south and the view of Downtown's skyline to the north are what put this causeway in a league of its own. A bona fide jogger's paradise, Rickenbacker Causeway's barricaded sidewalks offer a long stretch of safe and uninterrupted running space, while the bridge's steep inclines provide a much-needed break from the monotony of the area's otherwise level terrain – it's the only spot in town for hill training.

Start your day by hitting the ground running. Head to the causeway at sunrise to get your exercise in before the temperature spikes. The weather is also usually calmest at this hour, when the sun just breaks the horizon and illuminates Brickell's glittering skyline.

Address 3301 Rickenbacker Causeway, Miami, FL 33149 | Tip After your workout, reward yourself with an indulgence. End your morning run at the Rusty Pelican (3201 Rickenbacker Causeway). Enjoy the views of Biscayne Bay over a delicious brunch on the northeast tip of Virginia Key.

86 _ Robbie's
Fish feeding frenzy

Out at sea, reeling in a tarpon is a rare and unforgettable fishing experience for many amateur anglers. The massive silver fish are notorious for how much of a fight they put up and are known to leap completely out of the water, violently flailing above the surface, desperately trying to wriggle free of the hook. They'll dart in every direction imaginable, displaying their metallic sheen and huge, gaping mouths.

The legend of Robbie's began in 1976, when Robbie Reckwerdt spotted a struggling tarpon floundering in the shallows near his docks at the northeast corner of Lower Matecumbe. The beautiful green-and-silver creature had the right portion of its jaw torn apart, and Robbie was intent on saving it. So he called on his pal, Doc Roach, to patch up his finned friend using nothing but mattress needles and some twine. The operation was a success, and the newly dubbed "Scarface" was the first of many tarpon to come back and visit Robbie and company. At first, it was just Scarface and a few of his friends returning to the docks for some baitfish. But the word in the tarpon community seemed to spread like wildfire, and soon Robbie was overrun with fish. Robbie's old boat docks eventually became known as the place "where-you-feed-the-tarpon."

Grab a bucket of baitfish for a mere three dollars and get ready to have a ball. Lie prone on the docks, dangle a baitfish over the school of tarpon, and watch the madness ensue. Drop a piece in the water, and the tarpon will whip wildly around, trying to nab the tasty morsel. Hold the bait just above the surface and a fish will almost certainly jump out and eat it from your bare hands, possibly even engulfing your arm; there's no need to worry about getting bitten, though, as tarpon teeth are virtually nonexistent. At Robbie's docks, you can get nose to nose with hundreds of these giant creatures, without the boredom of waiting for a nibble on the open seas.

Address 77522 Overseas Highway, Islamorada, FL 33036, +1 305.664.8070, www.robbies.com | Hours Daily 8am–8pm | Tip A great place to go tarpon fishing is in the "blue water" just off Key West. A lot of the water surrounding the Keys is shallow and pale blue in color. A few miles offshore, the sea floor drops off, and the waters dramatically change from turquoise to navy.

87 Robert is Here

The little farm stand that could

A half hour due east of Brickell Avenue is a world outside Miami's sphere of influence. There is no beach, no eccentric skyline, no vibrant Hispanic culture or omnipresent glamour; no shopping malls, no convenience stores, no supermarkets, not even a Walmart. Instead, the Redlands are dominated by fields of fruits, vegetables, and legumes; humanity is sparse. The story of this bustling produce stand began in 1959, when Robert Moehling was just a first-grader selling cucumbers from his father's crop at the site where his fruit-and-vegetable mecca sits today. Despite Robert's initial efforts, nobody stopped to buy any cukes. His father assumed his six-year-old son was too small to be seen standing on the corner, so in order to increase visibility, he painted a huge sign with big red letters proclaiming ROBERT IS HERE. By noon the next day, Robert had sold all his father's cucumbers. Local farmers jumped on board by supplying little Robert with tomatoes, squash, and other produce to peddle. By the time he was nine, the business was doing so well he hired his first employee to run the stand while he was at school. And at the tender age of 14, Robert bought and maintained a 10-acre avocado grove, and sold his heart out.

Today, the old corner stand has exploded into a fruit-and-vegetable Valhalla. The name remains the same, but instead of a handwritten sign, tremendous white letters run across the roof. Florida's tropical fruit magnate expanded operations into a full store with a staggering selection of uniquely Floridian goods, ranging from orange blossom honey to alligator jerky. A crowd is always filtering through its doors, wandering the aisles looking for seasonal fruit butters, scouring the shelves for old-fashioned coconut patties, or waiting in line for a sumptuous milk shake. And Moehling is still at the helm after 50 years. "I've had the church of 'Robert is Here' since I was six years old," Moehling says. "Every Sunday. Every day."

Address 19200 SW 344th Street, Homestead, FL 33034, +1 305.246.1592, www.robertishere.com | Hours Nov–Labor Day, daily 8am–7pm | Tip While in Homestead, check out the Everglades Outpost (35601 SW 192nd Ave), a rescue and rehabilitation center for local and exotic animals. Director Bob Freer and his wife, Barbara, have cared for animals ranging from tigers and Florida panthers to grizzly bears and snakes since 1991.

88 Robert the Doll

Before there was Chucky, there was Robert

Inside an old Union fortress, built to protect Key West from Confederate assault during the Civil War, an equally terrifying and peculiar doll reclines in his chair with a small teddy bear. Over three feet in height, it once belonged to Robert Eugene Otto and is rumored to be enchanted, possessing mystical powers perhaps given to him by one of the Otto family's voodoo-practicing West-Indian servants. Robert the doll, stuffed with excelsior, stares blankly at passersby from within the confines of his Plexiglas chamber. At first glance, Robert seems innocuous enough, but the stories that surround his legacy are anything but.

The legend begins with Robert "Gene" Otto and a maid of Bahamian descent. In 1904, when Gene was a young child, it's said that his parents fired the maid for practicing "black magic," and before she left, she gave Gene the now infamously cursed doll to punish his family for their mistreatment of their servants. Gene soon named his new "friend" after himself, and the two became inseparable in the years that followed, although it may not have been a companionable relationship. There were nights where a screaming Gene woke up his family, and when they rushed in to see what was troubling him, they found his bedroom in disarray. Every time, he said, "Robert did it!" After multiple incidents, Gene's parents relegated the doll to the attic. When the house was sold to a new family, Robert the doll grew increasingly restless. There were reports of mysterious giggling coming from Gene's old room. Another description of an encounter even had Robert at the foot of a bed in the house, wielding a knife.

Today, Robert's mojo seems to have waned. In his new permanent residence at East Martello Tower, the only thing he asks of his admirers is to get his permission before taking his picture. Check the walls surrounding his display case and you'll find them covered with apology letters from the poor souls who took his picture without his approval.

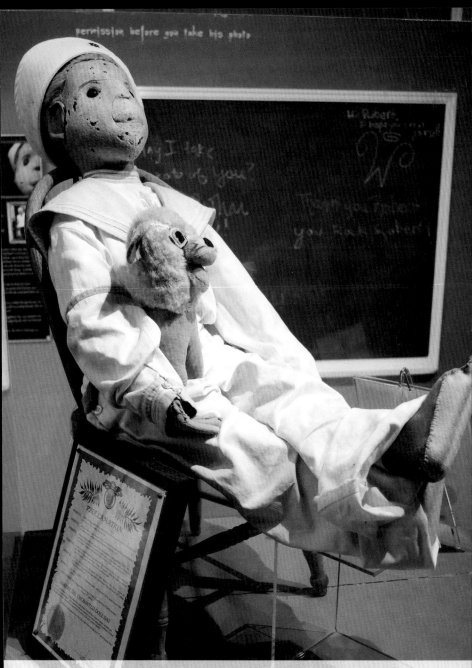

Address 3501 S Roosevelt Boulevard, Key West, FL 33040, +1 305.296.3913, www.kwahs.org/visit/fort-east-martello | **Hours** Daily 9:30am–4:30pm | **Tip** To reach Key West from Miami, you can drive over the waters via Overseas Highway – or you can fly. It's a quick flight – less than an hour – and is a scenic ride all the way. Snag a window seat and enjoy a spectacular aerial view of the Keys.

89__Schnebly Redland's Winery

No grapes necessary

A few blocks east of the Everglades, in a man-made oasis filled with coral rock and koi ponds, sits the southernmost winery in the contiguous United States. And there's not a grape to be found.

Beneath the intense Floridian sun, the only grapevines that can be grown and harvested are the extremely tart and acidic sea grapes indigenous to the area. Highly resistant to heat and salt, they're found lining the dunes of Miami's beaches. But making a palatable wine out of such a sweet-and-sour fruit is nearly impossible. Luckily, other fruits with greater sugar content, like mangoes and guavas, thrive in high temperatures and humidity. Best of all, someone's figured out how to turn their nectar into wine way out in the Redlands.

Before there was a winery, there was Peter and Denisse Schnebly's produce company, Fresh King. In the spring of 2003, their sommelier friend, Bill Wagner, came to town and hatched the idea to make wine from the tropical fruits they were harvesting. Months of fermentation and experimentation took place in the couple's garage, to determine what varieties would yield the best flavors. That fall, the winery was born.

The subtlety of traditional grape-based wines may be lost, but skeptical oenophiles should reserve judgment until they've tasted the bold, brash character of these exotic fruit wines. The syrupy lychee wine is similar in profile to a moscato or marsala – a perfect way to drink your dessert. The flavor of the mango wine is like a trip to the tropics, smooth with an air of sweetness. The avocado wine has a unique pungent odor, but the wine's pleasing nutty aftertaste more than compensates for it. The passion-fruit wine has the flavor of the infamous Warhead candy, featuring an intense sour kick followed by a sweet, fruity finish. The fragrance of the guava wine tickles the nostrils, an aromatic reminder that wine doesn't need grapes to be savored.

Address 30205 SW 217th Avenue, Homestead, FL 33030, +1 305.242.1224, www.schneblywinery.com | **Hours** Mon–Thu 10am–5pm, Fri–Sat 10am–11pm, Sun noon–6pm | **Tip** The winery is also home to Miami Brewing Company. Make sure to check out the brewing tanks and bottling machines, and perhaps grab a pint or two of their coconut ale.

90__Shark Valley

Everglades from above

Far away from the paved roads and shimmering megastructures of Downtown Miami, a flat, lush landscape dominates the field of view. Australian pines gently bend in the warm breeze. Cypress domes roll up on the horizon, growing in staggered heights from the marshy wetlands below. Shark Valley is the subtle geographic depression at the mouth of the Shark River, the gateway to one of the world's richest sanctuaries of biodiversity: the Florida Everglades.

During the dry season, the prairies are caked in limestone; the ground is like an abandoned, gray baseball diamond overrun with weeds. In the wet season, a shallow layer of water slowly trickles through the tall grass. Tropical hardwood hammocks appear like freshly popped green kernels, holding firm on the slightest rises in elevation. Twiggy, fragrant bayheads are full of aromatic bay leaves. Thick, bushy willowheads encase water-filled solution holes – smaller versions of sinkholes – that are home to the American alligator, the keeper of the Everglades.

The deeper into the Everglades you get, the more frequent the appearance of bushy shrubs and gator holes. The land is wetter, the saw grass and cattails grow thicker. In the distance, a unique vantage point for this densely packed biosphere stands above it all. The Shark Valley observation tower shoots through the horizon 45 feet up into the partly cloudy sky like Seattle's Space Needle. A spiral concrete walkway leads you to the top, where the panorama explodes all around you. The vastness of the grassy brown-and-green flatlands makes the viewer feel insignificant, swallowed by the tremendous expanse of vivacious flora and fauna. Great blue herons fly in the distance, gathering materials to build their nests. Alligators below bask in the sun, congregating en masse during the dry season. Mangroves line the waterways, which show no trace of human activity.

Address 36000 SW 8th Street, Miami, FL 33194, +1 305.221.8455, www.sharkvalleytramtours.com | Hours Dec 20–Apr, daily 9am–4pm, May–Dec 19, daily 9:30am–4pm | Tip Drive along Loop Rd in Ochopee and experience the Everglades from your car on arguably the loneliest stretch of road in the country. Largely unpaved and unkempt, it snakes through the old Florida wilderness, where alligators can be seen crossing the road and meandering through overgrown, abandoned settlements.

91 Shell World

They sell seashells by the seashore

A stroll along one of South Florida's many beaches is a different experience every time, not only because of the shifting tides or the position of the sun above the horizon. Sometimes just finding a new and peculiar shell or stone that's washed up on shore can be a game changer. Stumbling upon a small pink-and-white strawberry trochus shell, like a dirty strawberry ice cream cone in the sand, serves as a tactile reminder of a great day at the beach. Unfortunately, finding these colorful keepsakes requires hunting, and more than 50 years of industrial pollution has spawned the disappearance of some of the most beautiful and abundant species. If the effort to find the perfect shell ends up fruitless, drive over to Shell World, whose name says it all.

Whether you're in the market for a memento, starting a new craft project, or just have a shell fetish, you've come to the right place. Nary a native is found strolling the aisles of key chains and other stereotypically Floridian souvenirs inside Shell World. This place is certainly not lacking screened-on "Florida Keys" shirts and eight-count boxes of Key-lime coconut patties. But it's called Shell World, not Souvenir World, for a reason. Buckets, barrels, and shelves from floor to ceiling showcase every shell imaginable. Spiraling nautilus shells show off their beautiful orange-and-white stripes like undersea lollipops. Huge pink conch shells sit idly on a table, waiting for guests to hold them to their ears and listen for the sound of the ocean. Bins of blue pearlescent solarium shells, very similar to snail shells, shimmer under the lights. Starfish, sand dollars, and restored horseshoe-crab shells and carapaces are on display for the picking.

So when you're leaving the beach and heading home, stop off at Shell World, between the eastbound and westbound lanes of US 1 in the middle of Key Largo – and take a piece of the Keys with you.

Address 97600 Overseas Highway, Key Largo, FL 33037, +1 305.852.8245,
www.shellworldflkeys.com | Hours Daily 9am–8pm | Tip If you're willing to take the trip
to the southwest coast of Florida, the beaches on Sanibel Island, where the number of shells
seems to outnumber the grains of sand, are a sight to behold.

92 Skunk Ape Research Headquarters

Return of the Yeti

Much like Sasquatch lurks in the forests of the Pacific Northwest and the Abominable Snowman prowls the snowcapped Himalayas, a beast of similar ilk haunts the Everglades. The skunk ape, Florida's Bigfoot, is a humanoid, bipedal primate that supposedly stinks to high heaven. It's omnivorous, feasting on anything from indigenous flora like hog plums and leather ferns to fauna like lizards and wild hogs. In Ochopee, the skunk ape is more than just an urban legend; it has its own research center, cleverly disguised as an Everglades souvenir shop.

Growing up, resident skunk-ape expert and Everglades native David Shealy heard rumors of a creature covered in hair, standing upright, and smelling like a skunk. Since the tender age of 10, Shealy has dedicated his life to exposing this transient rapscallion, collecting immeasurable amounts of data and clues. According to Shealy, between seven and nine skunk apes exist in the Everglades, and he has recorded three confirmed sightings to date. Male skunk apes can reach seven feet in height and weigh up to 350 pounds, while females top out at six feet and 250 pounds.

You too can stalk the fleeting skunk ape, should you find yourself in Ochopee. Supposedly their habitat changes with the season. In the early fall, it's said they can be found in saw palmetto hammocks searching for berries, while in the winter, they're more likely to be seen in oak forests on the hunt for acorns. Their mating season is during the summer when the Everglades flood, so to increase your chances of a sighting, an elevated platform is suggested.

In the grand scheme of things, unfortunately, the odds of actually seeing a skunk ape are slim to none. Fortunately, a slice of old-fashioned, mysterious Americana still thrives in the remote wetlands of Collier County.

Address 40904 Tamiami Trail East, Ochopee, FL 34141, +1 239.695.2275,
www.skunkape.biz | **Hours** Daily 7am–6pm | **Tip** You're going to need fuel when hunting
for the elusive skunk ape. Stop by Joanie's Blue Crab Cafe (39395 Tamiami Trail E) and
enjoy some traditional Everglades fare. Try the Swamp Combo, complete with frog legs and
gator nuggets.

93 __ Skyline from Watson Island

A city on the rise

From the west side of Watson Island, where water from the Main Channel laps up onto the rocky shoreline, Miami's exploding skyline can be viewed from its most beautiful perspective. To the right, the iconic Freedom Tower punctures the sky like a syringe. The American Airlines Arena, home of the Miami Heat, glows red at dusk. By day, the sun's reflection dances through one of the country's largest glass-and-concrete labyrinths. By night, the illuminated causeways and skyline explain how the Magic City got its name.

After New York and Chicago, Miami has the largest number of high-rises that stretch above 500 feet. Although it's just the 44th largest city in America (more people live in Colorado Springs than Miami city proper), its skyline is among the country's most recognizable.

In a city teeming with unique buildings designed by world-class architects like Herzog & de Meuron, Morris Lapidus, and L. Murray Dixon, it's ironic that Miami's tallest skyscraper is the plain-looking, rectangular glass monolith of the Four Seasons Hotel. The second-tallest and most unmistakable silhouette in the skyline is the Southeast Financial Center. The 764-foot-tall chrome tower was built during Miami's once notorious cocaine trade. With its roof resembling the cubic pyramids from the old video game Q*bert, the building was the primary hub of the tremendous influx of drug money during the 1980s.

Since the new millennium, Miami has experienced an even bigger eruption of construction, thanks in part to the drug trade's fallout. Unlike New York and Chicago, Miami's skyline is relatively new; the majority of buildings were raised after 2000. And new development shows no sign of slowing anytime soon. For as many skyscrapers as there are populating the urban panorama, even more cranes hover above most of them.

Address 1000 MacArthur Causeway, Miami, FL 33132 | Tip If you happen to be on Watson Island during the day, visit Parrot Jungle (1111 Parrot Jungle Trail). Although the popular zoological park moved here from its original location in South Miami, it still offers a stunning variety of animals, from scarlet macaws to an albino alligator.

94__Skyward Kites

Go fly a kite

On the west side of Collins Avenue in North Miami Beach, a cool, salty breeze blows through throngs of naked sunbathers at Haulover's nude beach. If the reality of this scene is less attractive than the idea, the west side offers an equally colorful yet decidedly more innocent form of entertainment. There, against the backdrop of palm trees and the marina, slews of kites flap high in the sky, a nostalgic reminder of the carefree days of childhood.

At the foot of the marina's parking lot, a polychromatic collage of kites dangles from the awning of Miami's unofficial "kite-mobile." Owner Dan Ward set up shop at Haulover Park more than 20 years ago, starting out with a small 12-foot concession trailer in 1992. Generations of Miamians have visited Ward ever since; many of today's customers came here as kids and now bring their own children to experience the simple "unplugged" joy of flying a kite. Ward's original trailer has been replaced with a 28-footer, adorned with canopy tops and a tremendous selection of kites and windsocks that can be rented or bought outright.

Kites ranging from the size of a laptop computer to a hang glider all idly wait on the shelves for their chance to take to the winds. In the air flies everything from symbols of national pride to exotic fantasy. American flags soar alongside the black-and-green kites of the US Army. Octopus tentacles sway menacingly in the breeze, narrowly avoiding collision with a red-and-yellow Chinese dragon, whose long tail dances behind it.

A huge lawn rich with Florida's St. Augustine grass, otherwise known as crabgrass, is wide open, with plenty of room for a running start. Grab the kite by the mid-beam, sprint against the wind, release, and watch it go. Unravel the line from the spool and join the web of white strings crisscrossing the horizon. Frolic through the field and let go of your worries – but hold on tight to your kite!

Address Skyward Kites, Haulover Park, 10800 Collins Avenue, Miami Beach, FL 33154, +1 305.893.0906, www.skywardkites.com | Hours Daily 10am–sunset | Tip Head up Collins Ave (A1A) to Pier Park (18070 Collins Ave), where you'll find one of only two piers in Dade County. Pay five bucks to go fishing or grab a drink at the Beach Bar and relax on the neighboring sands.

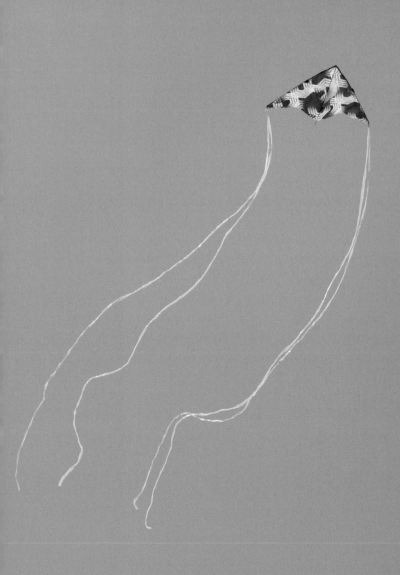

95 __ South Pointe Park

Sittin' on the dock of Biscayne Bay

The farther south you go in Miami Beach, the more vivacious it becomes. In the North, Haulover Beach attracts nudists working on their full body tans. The luxe shops at Bal Harbour lure wealthy customers from all over the world, while farther south, the Hasidic neighborhoods on Arthur Godfrey Road offer unique kosher cuisine, like a pareve chili cheese hot dog at House of Dog. Twenty-fourth Street marks the northern border of South Beach, and the transition is instantly noticeable. Art Deco buildings start popping up on every block; hotels and nightclubs, like the Clevelander and Story, dominate the bustling sidewalks of the avenues. But at the southern tip of Miami Beach, the commotion all but stops.

While most pedestrians push their way shoulder to shoulder along Ocean Drive and through Lummus Park, a quieter refuge lies just blocks away, at South Pointe Park. Originally opened in 1979, South Pointe was overhauled in 2009 by Hargreaves Associates, a San Francisco-based landscape architecture firm, turning it into a modern masterpiece of urban planning.

Where Lummus Park is a place to be seen, South Pointe Park is a place to see. The park's cutting-edge contemporary design is felt immediately upon entering. A promenade along Government Cut, lined with brushed-chrome lampposts, offers a uniquely up-close view of every type of boat imaginable floating through the inlet. Winding sidewalks on a hill at the park's center also feature a state-of-the-art amphitheater and a brilliant panorama, stretching from the beaches that border the Art Deco District to the docks at the Port of Miami, all seen from a rare elevated vantage point. The new 45-foot pier juts out into the Atlantic, punctuating the southern end of Miami Beach's eastern shoreline. Open every day from sunrise to sunset, it's the perfect place to cast a line or pause to take in the view.

Address 1 Washington Avenue, Miami Beach, 33139, +1 305.673, 7779, www.miamibeachfl.gov/parksandrecreation/scroll.aspx?id=57993 | Hours Daily sunrise–10pm | Tip One of the country's best steakhouses, Smith and Wollensky (1 Washington Ave), is on South Pointe Park's grounds. Eat your steak al fresco and watch the ships roll in and out of port.

96__ Southernmost Point

So they say …

The iconic Southernmost Point buoy at the southwestern corner of Whitehead and South Streets wasn't always the oft-photographed black, red, and yellow concrete mound it is today. Until 1983, the "Southernmost Point" was marked by a simple wooden sign that was stolen all too regularly. Key West's Conch Republicans put an end to that, replacing the flimsy marker with a virtually immovable, massive old sewer junction, painted over and disguised as a buoy. But just like the buoy isn't actually a buoy, the Southernmost Point isn't actually the southernmost point in Key West, let alone the contiguous United States.

Whitehead Spit, inaccessible due to its location on Key West's Naval base, reaches farther south than the buoy. But the Lower 48's true southernmost point is in Ballast Key, also inaccessible due to its being privately owned, nine miles west of Key West. (And while we're correcting fallacies, the buoy is technically 94 miles to Cuba, not 90.)

Somehow this misnomer epitomizes the peculiarity of Key West, which is popularly referred to as being "close to perfect, far from normal." Good times, not factual accuracy, are what matter most in this "anything goes" paradise, with its unabashed affinity for hedonism and creativity. From a clothing optional bar, fittingly called the Garden of Eden, to Hemingway's six-toed cats (see p. 116), to Mallory Square's bizarre street performers (see p. 44), to the fact that no one living here seems to have a last name but everyone has a nickname, the island's eccentricity is felt from end to end. These six oddball square miles of rock and coral sticking up in the Florida Straits even attempted to secede in 1982 as the Conch Republic, in typical Key West tongue-in-cheek fashion.

So just think of Key West as your cool, hippie, flip-flop-wearing uncle. He doesn't get his facts straight most of the time, but you can count on him spinning the most entertaining yarns.

Address Southwest corner of Whitehead and South Streets, Key West, FL, 33040 | Tip Take a journey to the Dry Tortugas, roughly 70 miles west of Key West, either by boat or seaplane. Dry Tortugas National Park, whose surrounding waters are largely untouched by civilization, are essentially the Galapagos of the States and home to nearly 300 species of exotic birds.

97__ Staircase to Nowhere
The Fontainebleau's folly

Miami Beach's oceanfront Fontainebleau Hotel has been the standard of luxury in South Florida for more than 60 years. The building was designed in 1954 by Miami's archduke of architecture, Morris Lapidus. Fleeing the pogroms in turn-of-the-century Russia as an infant, Lapidus locked in on pursuing the American Dream. Through the 1950s, he singlehandedly transformed Miami Beach from Lincoln Road to Temple Menorah, one real-estate project at a time.

Although the Fontainebleau is now considered the grande dame of Miami Beach, critics weren't so kind when it was newly built; views ranged from "boardinghouse baroque" to "superschlock" – from "high kitsch" to "pornography of architecture." The landmark hotel is as opulent as it is tremendous. In excess of 1,500 rooms are contained within the sparkling white megastructure, as well as more than ten restaurants and bars and a 40,000-square-foot spa. Its curved, sleek Miami-moderne exterior is unmistakable, but the interior, particularly the lobby, is what made the Fontainebleau's legend come alive.

Polished, white marble floors dotted with black marble bowties and punctured by modern Doric columns set the scene for the Chateau Lobby, whose ceiling drips with shimmering chandeliers shaped like upside-down wedding cakes, each 16 feet in diameter. But the centerpiece of the Fontainebleau's lobby is an alluring staircase that leads to nowhere.

At one time, the staircase led up to a coatroom. It was intended as a way for guests to be seen, fashionably ascending and descending the steps, showing off their regalia and posing for pictures. But with society becoming increasingly less formal, the desire to flaunt unnecessary furs in the warm climate dwindled. The coatroom was removed; the stairway, however, still remains, just as it was in 1954. Today it serves as an eccentric reminder of the way Miami Beach used to strut its stuff.

Address 4441 Collins Avenue, Miami Beach, FL 33140, +1 305.538.2000,
www.fontainebleau.com | Tip Lapidus's other famous Hotel, the Eden Roc
(4525 Collins Ave), borders the Fontainebleau. Check out the Fontainebleau's
smaller, slightly more subdued younger sister.

98__ Stiltsville

Square feet or square fathoms?

Looking out to Biscayne Bay from the mainland, a peculiar sight may catch your eye: seven buildings floating in the middle of the water, each raised on stilts, collectively known as Stiltsville. These hovering houses remain as a relic of the city's checkered past.

During prohibition, Miami was rife with speakeasies, but as quickly as they popped up, the cops found ways to close them down. A resourceful fisherman out of Key West came up with a brilliant idea. "Crawfish" Eddie Walker built a shack on stilts one mile offshore, where gambling was legal. There he served his famous chilau, crawfish chowder made from "the bottom scrapings of Biscayne Bay," as one customer described it. The shack was an instant hit. Two of Eddie's friends each built their own shack, and the legend of Stiltsville was born.

By 1960, there were 27 stilted houses in the middle of Biscayne Bay, including some used as bars and exclusive social clubs. Plush boat services sprang up to attract Miami's high society. It was – and still is – a gorgeous ride over shallow, calm waters to the shacks. It wasn't long before Stiltsville became the city's most exciting nightlife destination, offering everything from gambling to Mad Men-style ogling. While Miami Beach had the Playboy Club, Stiltsville had the Bikini Club – a grounded yacht in the middle of the bay that offered free drinks to any woman clad in a two-piece swimsuit, and provided a deck for nude sunbathing. Lacking a liquor license, the Bikini Club was shut down by the State Beverage Department in 1965.

Both the closure of the Bikini Club and the damage done by Hurricane Betsy in 1965 led to Stiltsville's inevitable demise, amid storms both tropical and legal. Not all was lost, though. Today, the remaining houses are still functional. The only way to get to them, however, is by navigating the shallows of Biscayne Bay by boat or kayak.

Address One mile south of Cape Florida on the edge of Biscayne Bay in Miami-Dade County, FL. Stiltsville can be reached by boat or kayak. Make rental inquiries at www.boatbound.com. The houses are only viewable from the outside. | Tip Abandoned objects of the sea are relatively common in South Florida and the Keys. At Bahia Honda State Park in the Keys (36850 Overseas Hwy) there's an old deserted rail bridge that's nestled on the corner of the island near the beach.

99 Stone Barge at Vizcaya

Party on a pirate ship

Vizcaya, James Deering's villa and estate turned museum and gardens in the northeastern corner of Coconut Grove, is the Versailles of the tropics. Deering (1859–1925) was a farming equipment magnate whose name could frequently be found in the social columns of the day. With his immense wealth came opulent taste. Magnificent landscaping surrounds the 30,000-square-foot Mediterranean revival mega-mansion built between 1914 and 1922 and furnished like a pre-Revolutionary French chateau.

Visitors often get lost in Vizcaya's gardens and interior. Many meander through the house with audio tours, while others stroll the grounds, admiring the blooming orchids neatly placed along geometric hedges and intricate moats. But a less frequently appreciated and equally decadent component of Vizcaya floats in the backyard, past the glistening pool and its luxurious grotto.

Appearing to be something between a marble dock and a Venetian battleship, an ornate breakwater known as "the barge" sits in the cove behind the villa. Tropical flora, fountains, statues, and even a teahouse were once housed on the stone barge. Today, the staircase and sides, coated with thin layers of green algae, are slowly being reclaimed by nature. During a tropical storm or on an unusually blustery day, the structure still protects the estate from getting battered by a rough chop. But in its heyday during the early 1920s, the barge also served as a magnificent party venue.

Alexander Stirling Calder, father of the famed 20th-century modern artist, sculpted the 158-foot breakwater adorned with mermaids, tritons, and Egyptian obelisks. During the barge's formative stage, portraitist John Singer Sargent visited Vizcaya and depicted Calder at work. It's said that when Deering deemed the mermaids' breasts on the front of the "ship" to be "too generous," it was Sargent who suggested they be resized to the more modest proportions seen today.

Address 3251 S Miami Avenue, Miami, FL 33129, +1 305.250.9133, www.vizcaya.org | Hours Wed–Mon 9:30am–4:30pm | Tip After a day at Vizcaya, spend a night with the University of Miami's jazz band. For an extraordinarily affordable experience in Coral Gables, visit Gusman Concert Hall (1314 Miller Dr) on the university campus and check their schedule of events.

100 Sunken Garden

Hidden beauty at Fairchild Tropical Gardens

People the world over travel to this lush enclave off Old Cutler Road to see the exquisite flora growing over the 83-acre plot of land that constitutes Fairchild Tropical Gardens. Ficus and banyans canopy much of the park, much like the surrounding neighborhood. As wonderful as the gardens are, spilling over with a rainbow of orchids and trellises covered in thick vines, the sheer amount of humanity roaming the park detracts from its natural beauty. At times, the grounds seem more like an attraction at Disney World than a preserve for exotic plants. This is especially true when Fairchild hosts an art installation by famed glass sculptor Dale Chihuly. The park becomes a Ken Kesey poster when Chihuly rolls in. His fantastical blown-glass pieces appear throughout the gardens – spherical orbs float in ponds, purple rods mingle with cacti, an exploding sunburst stands in the middle of a field.

But Fairchild's most coveted treasure is tucked away out of plain sight. The casual visitor may overlook this hidden oasis, instead following the concrete walking paths that snake through the park, drawn by the dramatic blooms of bromeliads. Near the cycad circle, an unmarked stair is hidden under the shade of a palm, well disguised in a maze of thick ferns. As you descend the broad steps, the light grows darker and the heat slowly dissipates. After a winding slope and a few more steps, the picture of tropical tranquility appears. An Elysian waterfall spills into the pond beneath, encased in coral rock, ferns, and gargantuan elephant-ear plants. A bench invites you to linger awhile in the cool air, removed from the crowds above.

By all means, enjoy the park to its fullest. Don't pass up the opportunity to ogle the tangled pygmy date palms or the deep reds of the firespike blooms. Just remember that beyond Fairchild's pretty face, her soul continuously pours from the waterfall in her sunken garden.

Address 10901 Old Cutler Road, Miami, FL 33156, +1 305.667.1651,
www.fairchildgarden.org | Hours Daily 9:30am–4:30pm, Thu and Sun open until 9pm |
Tip Check out Downtown's green space at Simpson Park Hammock (5 SW 17th Rd),
one of the last remnants of Brickell's tropical hardwood hammock. Venture inside its
modern pavilion designed by architect Chad Oppenheim.

101__ Sunrise at Crandon Park

Good morning, South Florida

New York, the city that never sleeps, has a fellow insomniac in Miami. There's the rush-hour commute to the office towers that line Brickell Avenue. Little Havana's engine revs early, powered by the sweet, caffeinated jet fuel its residents call *café*. South Beach is awash with sightseers all day and overflows with revelers all night, partying hard until the clubs shut down at 5am. In that small window between closing time and dawn, Miami stands still and takes a much-needed breath.

Sunrises are cheap in Miami. Straddling a picturesque stretch of the eastern seaboard, the city offers countless vantage points from which to glimpse the spectacle of night becoming day. For the ultimate front-row seat, there is no better spot than the tropical oasis of Crandon Park. By predawn, the park's sand beaches appear smooth and untouched, the previous day's evidence of humanity traversing the shoreline washed away overnight. Bring a blanket and a thermos of your favorite caffeinated brew and settle in for the show.

A live time lapse soon begins, as a glow as red as the Miami Heat's flaming basketball peeks up from the ocean and strikes the palms lining the shore. The horizon stitches the milky, reflective waters to the dim purples, reds, oranges, and blues of the sky above. The waters lap Key Biscayne's softest sands in near silence while an early-morning orchestra of light and the rising tide warm up, tuning their instruments in preparation for the new day. The song begins; the sky becomes a more pastel shade of blue with the gradual emergence of sunlight. The tempo quickens as the waters become more restless, mustering the energy to roll out of bed and up onto the beaches. The crescendo builds with the surfacing light, culminating with the sky set ablaze by the emerging sun. A spectrum from red to yellow shimmers on the ocean as the sun stretches its arms in a long, slow yawn. The South Beach partyers pass out, the Downtown workforce awakens, and the temperature, just like Miami, rises.

Address 6747 Crandon Boulevard, Key Biscayne, FL 33149, +1 305.361.5421, www.miamidade.gov parks/crandon.asp | Hours Daily sunrise – sunset | Tip As invigorating as the sunrise is over the Atlantic, the sunset into the Gulf of Mexico is as relaxing. Catch both: head for Key West after sunup to see the sunset festival at Mallory Square (400 Wall St), on the Key's northwest corner.

102__ Sweat Records

Vinyl and vegan

In the middle of Little Haiti, a purple-and-teal collage of some of the world's greatest pop stars is graffitied on a wall along Second Avenue. The robots of Daft Punk gaze blankly across the street, their faces covered by their notorious helmets. Prince looks to the heavens for the energy to belt out another one of his funky love tunes. The ageless Iggy Pop stares menacingly at passersby. Morrissey, formerly of the Smiths, bears his usual carefree smirk, his trademark hair flowing to one side. The sole window of the establishment is flanked by Notorious B.I.G., wearing the crown featured on his posthumous album *The Final Chapter*, and David Bowie as Ziggy Stardust, just back from Suffragette City.

Outside on the wall of the building, stars are immortalized; inside Sweat Records, vinyl has made its caffeinated comeback. As you enter its long, narrow interior, a petite coffee counter greets you with some of the best java in Miami, brewed with beans from Wynwood's Panther Coffee. A hipster establishment through and through, Sweat Records offers a bevy of vegan options, like the Unicorn Love Bomb (a double-shot of espresso topped with vegan marshmallows).

Sip your tea, coffee, or hot chocolate and peruse the vinyl that lines the maze of walls and aisles. The selection is astounding, ranging from a mint-condition press of the Beatles' *Magical Mystery Tour* to Miami's own 2 Live Crew's *As Nasty As They Wanna Be* to Mac DeMarco's *Salad Days*.

Sweat Records is also one of Miami's top destinations for live music. During events, the whole venue becomes a deep and narrow corridor jammed with throngs of 20-somethings who smell of Newport cigarettes. You definitely won't hear any Jimmy Buffett tribute bands or lounge acts. Sweat is dedicated to showcasing Miami's unique independent artists, and is a prime spot for loud, sweaty, and unforgettable standing-room-only gigs.

Address 5505 NE 2nd Avenue, Miami, FL 33137, +1 786.693.9309,
www.sweatrecordsmiami.com | **Hours** Mon–Sat noon–10pm, Sun noon–5pm | **Tip**
Head next door to Churchill's Pub (5501 NE 2nd Ave), where Sweat's crowd congregates
at night if there isn't a live show. The bar has all the essentials: pool tables, televisions, and
enough cold beer to sustain a small country for as long as needed.

103__ Theater of the Sea

Sea-life spectacle

Theater of the Sea was established in 1946 by P. F. McKenney, a tourist from Atlanta who was awestruck by the seaside beauty of Islamorada. After stumbling upon a flooded rock quarry filled with colorful parrotfish, he decided to buy the large lot of land for a "menagerie of sea critters." His vision was thoroughly realized, and remains owned and operated by his family to this day.

The grounds throughout the park are lush with tropical flora. Thick elephant-ear plants and bougainvillea line the paved paths, with occasional waterfalls trickling off to the side. The thickets clear and huge ponds come into view, teeming with some of the most colorful marine life on the planet. The neon green and magenta parrotfish that compelled McKenney to invest in his dream swim through the saltwater pools, under bridges, and occasionally come to the surface. Dolphins, sea turtles, nurse sharks, and seals swim just a few feet away from you in waters pumped in from the Atlantic.

You won't find tremendous aquariums on display with manatees and orcas, or massive stadiums that seat throngs of spectators here. Unlike many more modern venues of its type, Theater of the Sea is a small, independent establishment that provides visitors a much more intimate experience with the animals and encourages interaction; you can even swim with the dolphins!

But what also sets this marine mammal park apart is its ability to mimic the conditions of the neighboring ocean. Because of this, the facility meets the government's standards to house many protected species, like sea turtles, raptors, and crocodiles. Some marine animals here are rehabilitated and released back into the wild. Others, who can't return to their natural habitat, are given the opportunity to engage in natural behaviors by the staff's "enrichment" programs, which increase physical activity and promote social interaction.

Address 84721 Overseas Highway, Islamorada, FL 33036, +1 305.664.2431, www.theaterofthesea.com | Hours Daily 9:30am–3:30pm | Tip Snorkel or scuba dive into the natural habitats of many of Theater of the Sea's sea life. Less than a third of a mile down Overseas Highway, the Islamorada Dive Center (84001 Overseas Hwy) offers undersea tours, giving you the opportunity to see the aforementioned parrotfish and sea turtles in the wild.

104__ Venetian Pool
The emerald of Coral Gables

Before gated communities became en vogue in South Florida, there was Coral Gables, the meticulously planned and well-manicured subdivision of Miami. Otherwise known as the "City Beautiful," Coral Gables is recognized by many as Dade County's symbol for wealth and the urban planning it can buy. Street signs are molded concrete slabs less than a foot above the ground, every road is beautifully shaded by the banyan and ficus trees that line either side, and the homes are stitched together in a unique quilt; no one square is the same as the other. The Gables called for something more than an ordinary community pool, so something extraordinary is what they got.

In 1921, Coral Gables founder George Merrick, along with his uncle, artist Denman Fink, and architect Phineas Paist, repurposed an abandoned coral rock quarry into what was to become the Venetian Pool: the only public swimming pool in the country included in the National Register of Historic Places. Opened in 1924 as the Venetian Casino, it used to be a popular venue for music, featuring regular orchestral performances inside the drained pool, and public speaking events with notable celebrities.

Red iron gates enclose the landmark swimming palace, fit with coral bridges, underwater tunnels, towers with barrel-tile roofs, and streaming waterfalls. Lush, flowering ferns grow out of rocky crevices within the pool's caverns. Scraggly palm trees shoot up from the many floating islands, shrouded from outsiders by royal poincianas and bougainvillea. Pool-goers swim underwater and resurface in one of Venetian Pool's signature grottos, arguably the most coveted cool-off spots in the city. Besides its lavish Mediterranean revival design, the hydromechanics of the pool is a wonder in itself. The 820,000 gallons of spring water are drained, naturally filtered, and replenished daily from the Biscayne Aquifer.

Address 2701 De Soto Boulevard, Coral Gables, FL 33134, +1 305.460.5306, www.coralgables.com/index.aspx?page=167 | Hours Check website for exact dates, hours, and admission fees | Tip Visit the famous Biltmore Hotel (1200 Anastasia Ave). The Mission Revival building is rumored to be haunted by the ghost of Thomas Walsh, a New York mobster who was killed during a stay there.

105__ Versailles

A tale of two restaurants

From a distance, the beige castle on Calle Ocho is shrouded by a dense field of cars. A huge white sign reading "Versailles Restaurant: Cuban Cuisine" in green letters hovers high above, demanding respect for the chrome interior that awaits. Kelly green vinyl-upholstered diner chairs and tables fill the establishment by the hundreds, arranged atop sparkling white tile and beneath a mirrored ceiling. But Versailles is known by many as more than just a great restaurant: it is also a must-stop on the campaign trail for any politician seeking the Cuban vote.

In 1971, Versailles opened its doors and became the unofficial meeting place for Little Havana's Cuban exiles, plotting and scheming different ways to overthrow Fidel Castro. In less than two decades, the restaurant evolved from a simple Cuban eatery to a national political tipping point. As the Cuban population grew, so did the power of their vote. Candidates needed this key demographic to have any hope of getting elected to office, especially in Florida. Over the years, political heavyweights, the likes of President Bill Clinton and former Florida governor Jeb Bush, have visited Versailles to both do some glad-handing and grab a bowl of arroz con pollo.

By day, the legendary eatery is Miami's kingmakers' hangout, but late at night, Versailles loosens its tie and undoes its belt a notch. The scene changes from political incubator to brazen Cuban diner, serving dish after dish of the best late-night munchies in the 305 to grumbling stomachs in desperate need of a post-mojito meal. The South Beach Diet stays on South Beach, as tipsy patrons, wandering in after a long night of cocktails and salsa dancing, devour crisp-fried gooey ham-and-cheese croquetas and sweet-and-savory *medianoche* sandwiches like they haven't seen food in days. For those still struggling to regain their equilibrium, a Hail Mary in the form of a cortadito should do the trick.

Address 3555 SW 8th Street, Miami, 33135, +1 305.444.0240, www.versaillesrestaurant.com | **Hours** Mon–Thu 8am–1am, Fri 8am–2:30am, Sat 8am–3:30am, Sun 9am–1am | **Tip** If you're looking for Cuban food in South Beach, head to Puerto Sagua (700 Collins Ave). Puerto Sagua is more laid-back than Versailles, so dress casually and enjoy an Elena Ruz or two.

106 Virginia Key Beach Park
The long arm of Jim Crow

For the first 70 years of its existence, Miami wasn't exactly the cultural melting pot it is today. Easily forgotten in the cosmopolitan and ethnic mix that's swallowed the city is the fact that Miami was once of the Old South. Like Birmingham, Atlanta, and Jackson, it enforced the notorious Jim Crow laws. It was mandated that minorities use separate bathrooms, restaurants, drinking fountains, movie houses – even beaches.

In fact, all of Miami Beach was segregated for the majority of the 20th century. The first beach that allowed people of color was Fisher Island. In 1918, African-American millionaire D. A. Dorsey bought it in order to give blacks a beach of their own. Dorsey was a Georgia native who made his fortune providing housing for black railroad workers in South Florida. But shortly after he purchased Fisher Island, property taxes increased, and Dorsey sold the land only a year and a half after he bought it. It would take another 25 years before Miami officially created a separate beach for African Americans.

On August 1, 1945, Bear Cut at Virginia Key Beach was formally designated "for exclusive use of Negroes." Miami's rapid urban development hadn't yet taken hold, and Virginia Key was still completely separated from the mainland, accessible only by boat. Local black fishermen would ferry beachgoers to and from Virginia Key, but if anyone was unfortunate enough to miss the last boat back at the end of the day, they had to stay overnight and wait for the first boat to arrive the following morning. In 1947, Virginia Key was finally connected to the mainland and Key Biscayne by the newly constructed Rickenbacker Causeway.

Like the rest of the South, following the Civil Rights movement in the early 1960s, Virginia Key Beach slowly became integrated. Today, an amalgam of Miami's diverse population lines its shore.

Address 4020 Virginia Beach Drive, Miami, FL 33149, +1 305.960.4600, www.virginiakeybeachpark.net | Hours Daily 7am–sunset | Tip Grab a drink at one of Miami's most elusive bars, Wetlab (4600 Rickenbacker Causeway), on Key Biscayne. Open only Wednesdays and Thursdays from 5pm to 9pm and Fridays from 4:30pm to 11pm, Wetlab sits right on the sand and is a hangout for many University of Miami students.

107__Wallcast

An orchestra for the everyman

The New World Symphony, the only full-time orchestral academy in the country, is a hotbed of up-and-coming virtuosos – and you can see them, al fresco, at the futuristic SoundScape at New World Center. Bring a blanket, cheese, and some wine, and spend the night relaxing on the concert hall's lawn in the heart of Miami Beach, while a live projection of a world-class symphony is displayed on the 7,000-square-foot exterior wall of the building.

The technology is cleverly disguised in weblike modern art sculptures, with 160 loudspeakers surrounding the audience outside, transmitting the slightest flutter of a piccolo or tremolo of a cello from microphones inside. As sophisticated as the hardware is, its replication of the actual acoustics from within the hall itself makes it truly paramount.

Arriving early is a must if you want to get a good spot. Palm fronds dot the field of view from many vantage points, so prime, unobstructed seats get snatched up quickly. Once you're settled, it's time to break out the refreshments and strike up some conversation to pass the time. It's an informal social hour before the show, much like the pre-symphony cocktail hour in the lobby, but with picnics, children, and the occasional dog running by. As dusk creeps in, the ambient lights flick off and the Wallcast concert begins.

Renowned conductor Michael Tilson Thomas greets both the audience in the New World Center theater and those watching from the lawn, creating an inclusive, intimate atmosphere. Once the music begins, the camera pans the orchestra, guiding viewers to the highlights of the performance. Stay as long as you want or enjoy the freedom of being able to move on to dinner or a club without disturbing other concertgoers. Equal parts drive-in movie theater, Grateful Dead concert, and a pastoral day at Tanglewood, a Wallcast show is a uniquely low-key, sophisticated affair; and best of all – it's free of charge.

Address 500 17th Street, Miami Beach, FL 33139, +1 305.673.3330, www.nws.edu/wallcasts | Hours Oct–Apr; check website for performance schedule | Tip In the heart of Miami Beach, New World Center is surrounded by restaurants. Grab the essentials pre-show at a nearby eatery that suits your fancy. Rosinella (525 Lincoln Rd) is a great place to snatch up a bottle of wine and some antipasto to go.

108__Wat Buddharangsi
Serenity now

In 1982, the Thai Embassy sent a Buddhist monk named Ajarn Surachett to the States in order to establish a sanctuary of peace and meditation for the small Thai Buddhist community in Miami. In 1986, five acres in Homestead near a Mennonite settlement were acquired as the building site. In 2002, having weathered a storm of hardships that included inadequate funding, blueprint revisions, and Hurricane Andrew, Surachett finally completed Wat Buddharangsi: the Theravada Buddhist palace of Dade County.

Only 45 minutes from Downtown Miami, this spiritual retreat offers solace and relief from the grind of the city. The Buddhist temple is an anomaly not only in the rural town of Homestead, but is also the only one if its kind in the entire county. The grounds more closely resemble Bangkok than South Beach; the temple's glowing white facade is adorned with traditional gold trimmings shipped over from Thailand. Barefoot monks stroll the property in bright orange robes until the bell rings, signifying the time for meditation or to receive teachings in the sacred building's great room. There you will find the grand cynosure, a 23-foot, 5-ton bronze statue of Phrabuddhadhammachinaraj, the buddha of Wat Buddharangsi, which arrived in Miami in 1997. Among the golden statues and burning candles, visitors are invited to take their shoes off, have a seat on the orange carpet, and meditate.

The temple serves both visitors who want to talk with the monks that call Wat Buddharangsi their home, and those who are simply looking for a tranquil moment of solitude. The temple offers meditation teachings every Sunday from 3pm to 5pm, which are free to the public. On special Buddhist holidays, they host weekend retreats devoted to practicing the eight Buddhist precepts, offering a unique opportunity to free yourself of desires and *just be*, even if only for a day or two.

Address 15200 SW 240th Street, Homestead, FL 33032, +1 305.245.2702, www.thaitemplemiami.com | Hours Daily 7am–5pm | Tip There are guided meditations and classes available at the Drolma Kadampa Buddhist Center (1273 Coral Way, Miami) near Downtown. Resident teacher Gen Kelsang Norbu was ordained as a monk in 2006 by the Tibetan-born master Geshe Kelsang Gyatso Rinpoche.

109__Wolfsonian

Mediterranean marshmallow

Two blocks from South Beach, in the middle of the historic Art Deco District, sits a seven-story Mediterranean white cube with gold trimmings that resembles an enormous, extravagant marshmallow. Mitchell Wolfson Jr.'s warehouse-turned-museum is the city's most eccentric collection of tchotchkes and masterpieces alike, featuring items ranging from a pre-war German coffeemaker to a self-portrait of Spanish painter Federico Castellon. Inside, a visual history of modern international society is displayed floor by floor.

For most of its existence, what's now the Wolfsonian was the Washington Storage Company, a place where Miami Beach's wealthy kept their valuables during the summer months when they headed back north. Wolfson stored many of his unique objects in the facility, eventually occupying over 90 percent of its space. He finally bought the building, transforming it into a showcase for his diverse collection.

A shimmering fountain greets visitors at the end of the entryway, with water slowly spilling out from underneath a magnificent depression-era window grille. Standing roughly 15 feet high, it's fit with gold flowers and green-painted leaves, built from more than 100 glazed terra-cotta tiles. The walls flanking the fountain read "Lo and behold" on one side and "Mira & ve" on the other, foreshadowing the museum's tone right off the bat. To the left of the fountain, a grand elevator with a vintage floor indicator becomes your chauffeur to the upstairs galleries.

The evolution of technology in the modern era is featured throughout the museum, but all exhibits are fleeting. One weekend you might find early 20th-century typewriters, cash registers, radios, and televisions on the fifth floor. Return another day, and you'll discover political propaganda posters from 1970s Afghanistan. Its collection is just like the city it represents: eclectic and constantly changing.

Address 1001 Washington Avenue, Miami Beach, FL 33139, +1 305.531.1001, www.wolfsonian.org | **Hours** Mon–Tue, Thu, Sat 10am–6pm, Fri 10am–9pm, Sun noon–6pm | **Tip** Punctuate a day at this eclectic museum with some equally eclectic Colombian fare at La Perrada de Edgar (6976 Collins Ave). Order up one of their whacky hot dogs, like the Edgar Special, topped with mozzarella cheese, various fruits, and whipped cream.

110 — Wood Tavern's Bathrooms
Art surrounds the throne

From I-95, Wynwood looks like something out of an R. Crumb poster. Just beyond the concrete median and metal guard rail, sandwiched between Little Haiti and Overtown, sits a gritty fairy tale steeped in spray paint and sorcery. Within its borders, everything and everybody is covered in graffiti and ink. Emanating from the landmark walls in the middle of the neighborhood, this exquisite epidemic of public art cannot be contained. Not even the bathrooms are safe in Wynwood.

Wood Tavern is clearly no exception. The laid-back vibes from this local watering hole not only embrace the public art scene, but also attract it. After a long day of transforming a rare plain wall into a masterpiece, the youth of Wynwood flocks to Wood Tavern to decompress. The craft IPAs, Belgians, and porters flow all night into the mouths of thirsty artists and young urbanites.

After a few pints, one might have to get up from the tastefully vandalized picnic table and head to the little virtuoso's room. In a dingy hallway bordered by kegs supplying the tavern's lifeblood sits a row of doors that conjures up images of an edgier *Let's Make a Deal*. Instead of a brand-new car or a bag of potting soil, behind these doors lie the ravishing unisex restrooms of Wood Tavern, featuring surprisingly immaculate toilets. What steals the show isn't the clean commodes, but the rooms they're situated in. Like microcosms of the neighborhood, these restrooms are living, breathing, albeit odorous, public art exhibitions. Unregulated art is expressed on the walls many times over with tags, murals, stickers, and anything else that Wood's bathroom-goers can admire.

Relieve yourself in a spectacular reprise. These vandalized johns are a sight to see while doing unsightly things. After doing your business, head back to the bench, order a few more rounds of Wynwood La Rubias, and repeat.

Address 2531 NW 2nd Avenue, Miami, FL 33127, +1 305.748.2828, www.woodtavernmiami.com | Hours Tue–Sat 5pm–3am, Sun 3pm–11pm | Tip After a few cocktails at Wood Tavern, wander through the graffitied jungle of Wynwood, whose spray-painted murals engulf the entire neighborhood.

111__World Erotic Art Museum

The Smithsonian of kink

Two blocks inland from Miami's famous Art Deco District sits a museum that captures the essence of the city's lack of inhibition. Do not be fooled: this is not a showcase for pornography; items ranging from ancient Egyptian fertility amulets to the phallic murder weapon from Kubrick's *A Clockwork Orange* are presented just as any valuable object would be in a traditional museum.

The World Erotic Art Museum was founded by Naomi Wilzig. The wife of Siggi Wilzig, a Holocaust survivor and banker, Mrs. Wilzig collected erotica from 1983 until her death in 2015. It all started when her son asked her to find a "sexy conversation piece" for his new bachelor pad. The collection came to exceed 4,000 pieces.

The museum's entryway is at street level, but you have to take an elevator to the second floor to reach the exhibition space, just out of sight from the prying eyes of pedestrians. A "sperm bank," in the same vein as a piggy bank, is on sale next to the receptionist. In the main gallery are works of art ranging from Disney characters engaging in lascivious acts to a detailed cast of a vulva in plaster. Straight ahead, in the homoerotic room, there's a golden eight-foot penis sculpture that doubles as a chair (with an actual seat, mind you). In the next gallery, a giant "Kama Sutra Engraved Bed," carved in Germany around 1990, features four phallic-shaped posts and 138 sexually explicit carvings. The museum also has an abundance of female genitalia on view. One relief depicts 16th-century Chinese women, made from mother of pearl, bathing in the nude on an onyx canvas. In the same room, a life-sized copper statue of a naked female figure, doing what looks like a headstand, is covered in rhinestones.

The World Erotic Art Museum exists to make its guests reevaluate their most primal urges. Here, the id learns some manners.

Address 1205 Washington Avenue, Miami Beach, FL 33139, +1 305.532.9336, www.weam.com | Hours Mon–Thu 11am–10pm, Fri–Sun 11am–midnight | Tip The Miami Beach Cinematheque (1130 Washington Ave) is a half block south of the museum. There you can watch independent and international films in what was once City Hall.

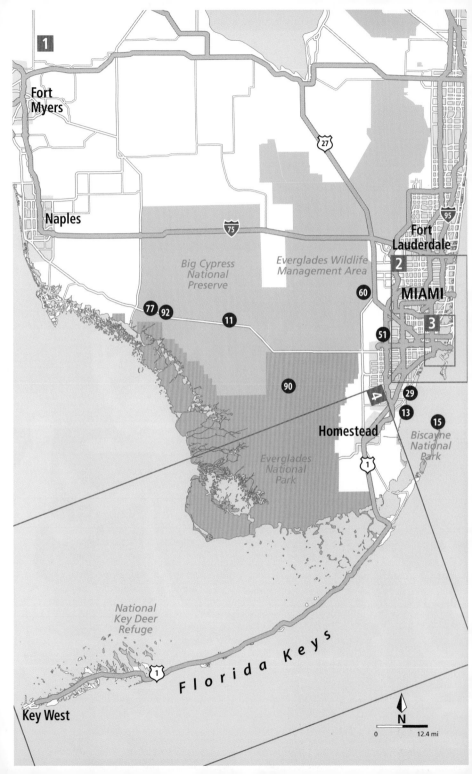

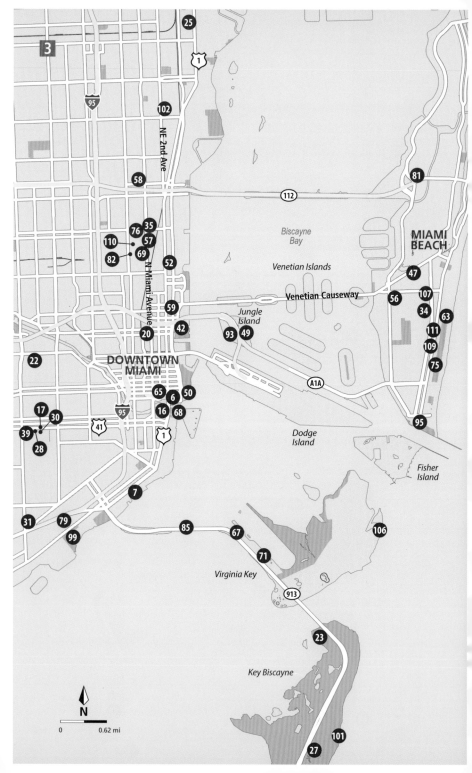

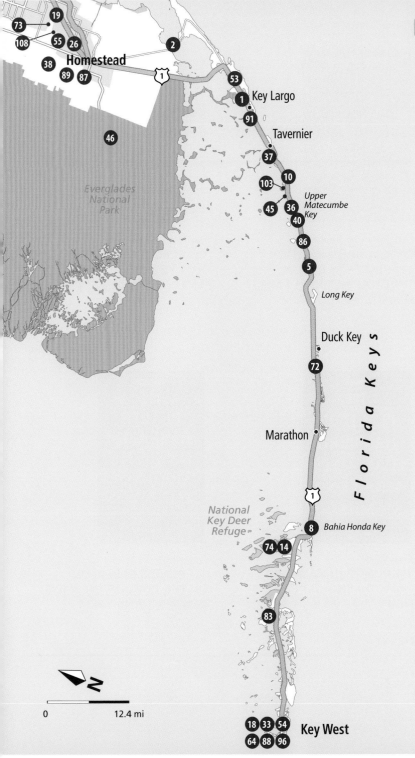

4

Lucia Jay von Seldeneck,
Carolin Huder, Verena Eidel
**111 PLACES IN BERLIN
THAT YOU SHOULDN'T MISS**
ISBN 978-3-95451-208-9

Rüdiger Liedtke
**111 PLACES IN MUNICH
THAT YOU SHOULDN'T MISS**
ISBN 978-3-95451-222-5

Rike Wolf
**111 PLACES IN HAMBURG
THAT YOU SHOULDN'T MISS**
ISBN 978-3-95451-234-8

Paul Kohl
**111 PLACES IN BERLIN
ON THE TRAIL OF THE NAZIS**
ISBN 978-3-95451-323-9

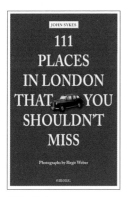

John Sykes
**111 PLACES IN LONDON
THAT YOU SHOULDN'T MISS**
ISBN 978-3-95451-346-8

Dirk Engelhardt
**111 PLACES IN BARCELONA
THAT YOU MUST NOT MISS**
ISBN 978-3-95451-353-6

Peter Eickhoff
**111 PLACES IN VIENNA
THAT YOU SHOULDN'T MISS**
ISBN 978-3-95451-206-5

Michael Murphy, Sally Asher
**111 PLACES IN NEW ORLEANS
THAT YOU MUST NOT MISS**
ISBN 978-3-95451-645-2

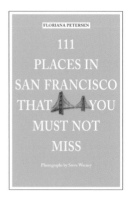

Floriana Petersen, Steve Werney
**111 PLACES IN SAN FRANCISCO
THAT YOU MUST NOT MISS**
ISBN 978-3-95451-609-4

Marcus X. Schmid
**111 PLACES IN ISTANBUL
THAT YOU MUST NOT MISS**
ISBN 978-3-95451-423-6

Ralf Nestmeyer
**111 PLACES IN PROVENCE
THAT YOU MUST NOT MISS**
ISBN 978-3-95451-422-9

Christiane Bröcker,
Babette Schröder
**111 PLACES IN STOCKHOLM
THAT YOU MUST NOT MISS**
ISBN 978-3-95451-459-5

Gerd Wolfgang Sievers
111 PLACES IN VENICE
THAT YOU MUST NOT MISS
ISBN 978-3-95451-460-1

Petra Sophia Zimmermann
111 PLACES IN VERONA
AND LAKE GARDA THAT
YOU MUST NOT MISS
ISBN 978-3-95451-611-7

Annett Klingner
111 PLACES IN ROME
THAT YOU MUST NOT MISS
ISBN 978-3-95451-469-4

Jo-Anne Elikann
111 PLACES IN NEW YORK
THAT YOU MUST NOT MISS
ISBN 978-3-95451-052-8

Acknowledgements

Writing this book would not have been possible if it weren't for the following, who I am deeply indebted to: My supremely talented editor, Katrina Fried, who has pushed me to become a better writer; Amy Hertz, without whose help this book would have not been possible; my father and stepmother, Mark and Sandra, for their invaluable input. My mother and stepfather, Melissa and John, for all their support. My grandparents, Jane and Barney, for giving me insight on the Miami of yore. And last but not least: Sammy Leigh, John, Turi, Ann, Jack, and Sam – thank you for giving me the best company I could ask for on a roadie.

Author and Photographer

Gordon Streisand is a third-generation Miami native whose family has called Miami and the Keys home since the now dwarfed courthouse was the tallest building in the city. A graduate of the University of Florida in Gainesville, Gordon has been a sportswriter and columnist and enjoys sharing the lesser-known wonders of his hometown with visitors of all types and ages.